One Environment
Under Law

**GOODYEAR SERIES IN AMERICAN POLITICS AND PUBLIC POLICY**
**Joel B. Grossman, Series Editor**

RACIAL EQUALITY IN AMERICA: IN SEARCH OF AN UNFULFILLED GOAL
Charles S. Bullock, III and Harrell R. Rodgers, Jr.

ONE ENVIRONMENT UNDER LAW: A PUBLIC-POLICY DILEMMA
Lettie McSpadden Wenner

CONTINUITY AND CHANGE: FROM THE WARREN COURT TO THE BURGER COURT
Stephen L. Wasby

# One Environment Under Law

## A Public-Policy Dilemma



LETTIE McSPADDEN WENNER
University of Illinois at Chicago Circle

Goodyear Publishing Company, Inc.
Pacific Palisades, California

**Library of Congress Cataloging in Publication Data**

Wenner, Lettie McSpadden.
One environment under law.

(Goodyear series in American politics and public policy)
Includes bibliographical references and index.
1. Environmental law—United States. 2. Environmental policy—United States.
I. Title
KF3775.W46 301.31′0973 75-19567
ISBN 0–87620–642–9



Library of Congress Catalog Card Number: 75-19567

ISBN: 0-87620-642-9
Y-6429-8

Current Printing (last digit):
10 9 8 7 6 5 4 3 2 1

Printed in the United States of America

To Donald Meiklejohn, an undergraduate's inspiration

# Contents

# Preface

Of the numerous books and articles that have recently appeared on environmental-policy problems, many have viewed problem analysis and policy prescription from an economic rather than from a political perspective. Most of the latter have focused on the direction toward which policy ought to be heading and have prescribed its path. This book will not plead for yet another "solution" to the environmental-degradation problem but will briefly lay out the problems that environmental control presents for the policy maker, the methods by which the U.S. government has formerly and currently attempted to deal with these problems, and will then draw some distinctions among the various proposed solutions.

The parts of this book are designed to perform three separate functions. The first section, Public Policy: Definitions, explains my own approach to public-policy problems, with emphasis on the political aspects. Using environmental laws and regulations as examples, it explains how issues become politicized and acted upon by governmental agencies. Although the National Environmental Policy Act is explained in detail, there is no intention to emphasize any level or branch of government over the others. The purpose of this first part of the book is to present a broad overview of how the machinery of government works to create policy in any issue area. Throughout the remainder of the book, when particular policies are discussed, it is hoped that the reader will draw on the framework created in this section to understand what has happened with regard to specific environmental policies.

The middle section, Environmental Policy Today, is the largest of the three, it being one of my contentions that descriptions of this policy problem and prescriptions for change have glossed over policy makers' actual dealings with the problem. This is understandable, and in some ways very wise strategy, given the constantly shifting state of the government's environmental policy and the difficulties involved in keeping abreast of such a complex field. If predicting the next stage of the formulation of this policy is difficult, it is nevertheless possible to make some generalizations about the direction toward which policy has developed in the past, and an effort has been made to do so in this middle section, Part 2. I have consciously emphasized the circularity of the policy process and the continual evolution of environmental policy.

I am certainly no exception to the rule that no author comes to this policy problem neutral. I do not, however, suggest a panacea for the problem; in fact, I advocate a critical review of all suggested solutions because of the general lack of empirical evidence for their capacity to change policy outcomes. In Part 3, therefore, no choices have been made among the various allegations of blame and suggestions for change, although the reader will identify my proclivity for political variables and political considerations.

My major purpose in Part 3 is to lead the discerning reader to make his own judgments concerning the utility of the arguments set forth in this part. I do not expect the proponents of any given solution to be satisfied with my brief description of their ideas. I merely present the general reader and the newcomer to this field with an overview of the richness and variety of suggestions for reform that exist in this policy area. In every case there are more eloquent statements of the arguments and I have indicated where to find some of these.

This brief survey of the environmental-policy area will prove useful not only to persons who are interested in the environment as an important subject for constant governmental attention but also to those general students of public-policy analysis who wish to deal with concrete examples. It is intended for use in both environmental-policy courses for undergraduates and general policy-analysis courses.

In the course of preparation of this book I have incurred the normal number of intellectual debts. I have been influenced by individual stances taken with regard to policy analysis in my graduate training at the University of Wisconsin, including those of Murray Edelman, Herbert Jacob, and Ira Sharkansky. I have had the benefit of teaching an environmental-politics course to students at the University of Illinois at Chicago Circle, whose insightful questions and arguments have broadened my views on many subjects. Over the years I have had the benefit of many enjoyable and informative conversations with officials who are active practitioners of environmental policy on the local, state, and federal levels. It is because of their generosity in giving of their time and information that this book is possible. I am also indebted to colleagues who reviewed earlier versions of this manuscript, including Boyd Keenan and Leslie Roos, Jr. Anita Worthington performed efficiently the difficult task of creating a legible manuscript from my copy and Janice Gallagher copyedited this manuscript into a readable book, for which I am most grateful. My largest debts, however, are to the editor of this series, Joel Grossman, and to my husband, Manfred W. Wenner, for their constant encouragement and editorial skills.

PART 1

# Public Policy: Definitions

CHAPTER ONE

# The Environment: Subject for Governmental Action?

## A PARABLE

An eccentric, elderly man living in an affluent suburb, not having much else to occupy his time, grew a large vegetable garden each summer as a hobby. One spring he decided to increase his crop yield by using the traditional method employed by his father on their family acreage years ago to add to the fertility of his soil.

He bought a large quantity of cow dung and spread it liberally over the garden area that comprised most of his backyard. His neighbors, whose new and elaborate dwellings overlooked the elderly man's manure pile, became incensed at this olfactory intrusion and complained indignantly to the public-health authorities in their municipality. They were subsequently gratified when a police car arrived and uniformed officers informed the gentleman that he would either have to bury the turds or have the city do it for him and sue him for reimbursement.

Later the same year these suburbanites in their fine new environment raked up dead leaves and with nostalgia for their own childhood, when autumn meant leaf piles and pumpkins, watched them burn and inhaled the fumes. One unfortunate inhabitant of the same area, however, a sickly ten-year-old afflicted with allergic reactions to almost all growing things, animal or vegetable, had an asthmatic attack upon inhaling these fumes, was rushed to the hospital, and spent several days in an oxygen tent at great expense to his widowed mother. The latter tried to convince the law-enforcement authorities, who had previously responded so readily, to help her establish grounds for a civil suit against her neighbors. The officials reluctantly admitted the existence of an aged city ordinance against open burning but asserted that the ordinance had not traditionally been called into effect for mere leaf burning and had been designed for more unusual events such as the incineration of large piles of rubber tires. When pressed, they declared that the evidence was now cold, that they could not be expected to act on a complaint several weeks old, and that they would have to be called out at the time of the incident, as in the case of the elderly manure spreader. No action was taken.

To all appearances, a specific law (against open air burning) did not provide a remedy for leaf burning, but a general one (public nuisance) coerced the spreader of manure into altering his behavior. Is it correct to conclude that the public policy of our imaginary suburb condones the burning of leaves and condemns the use of natural fertilizers? If so, the question remains whether publicly proclaimed policy as stated in city ordinances can be taken at face value—whether these laws in fact represent public policy. Do official statements have any effect on the actual administration of programs, and do these in turn have any impact on the actual environment? If all discretion rests with the enforcers, is the "real" public policy found in discernible patterns of environmental-law enforcement?

Some of the kinds of problems with which we shall be concerned in this book are: What constitutes public policy? How is it formulated? How is it changed? What relationship is there between formal pronouncements of policy and actual official and individual behavior? To what degree does public demand shape public policy in this area? In addition to such empirical questions, the two preceding examples of air pollution and its control by the authorities illustrate many traditional dilemmas of democracy: Are the rights of individuals to dispose of their leaves or to fertilize their gardens more or less important than the rights of those whom they offend or injure through their actions? Who was the more grievously injured party, the property owners who suffered an awakening of their olfactory senses or the child who suffered physical pain and whose mother suffered economic loss? Is a serious injury to one or two people equated with or considered to outweigh a minor annoyance to a larger group of householders? If the single offender was made to conform to the demands of his neighbors, should not the other set of offenders have also been controlled in some way? How can two entirely different grievances receive fair treatment at the hands of the same governmental authority?

Is it possible to determine what constitutes the "public good" in these two cases? If the majority of residents approve of leaf burning and disapprove of manure spreading, should authorities ignore the former and control the latter? What then happens to the rights of minorities—elderly gardeners and asthma sufferers who are allergic to tree pollen? Underlying these questions concerning individual justice is the broader normative question: What is the proper role for government in such conflicts? If control of the environment is a legitimate function for governmental agencies to undertake, what kinds of programs should they administer?

## WHAT IS PUBLIC POLICY?

The distinction between public policy and matters best left to private decision makers has long been a subject for debate. From the many divergent descriptions of public policy I shall adopt a simple one—"what government chooses to do or not to do."[1] The subjects subsumed under this definition of public policy should not seem arbitrary or capricious. Programs initiated and carried out by different governments during different periods in history still have their similarities. There are also easily identifiable goods and services, such as adequate protection against muggers, fire, or even foreign invasion, that most private citizens seem incapable of providing for themselves. There are others, such as education and garbage collection, that lend themselves to economies of scale. The public sector can provide these amenities at a level that few individual-family units can rival.

This is not to imply, however, that only those programs implemented by governments for centuries are worthy of consideration as legitimate targets of public policy; nor is it to say that any ongoing governmental policy is self-evidently applicable to all people in all places. We assume that government acts in accordance with the desires of at least the politically powerful portion of its population. No government is above, below, or in any way beyond the expressed wishes of some part of its citizenry that is motivated by its own physical needs. The governors of a country in which half the staple crops are destroyed yearly by locusts will have an active interest in pest control, whereas one facing imminent foreign invasion will devote a larger amount of its public resources to national defense. All governments face internal disintegration if they are not minimally responsive to at least some portion of the polity, and we may assume that the increasing interest exhibited by all levels of government in pollution control both in the United States and in other developed countries reflects an increasing demand for action from some segment of the population.

Any debate over the initiation or expansion of public policy will include discussion of the legitimacy of governmental involvement in the entire subject. Until recently both individual polluters and private industry have steadfastly defended their right to dispose of wastes in the physical environment without governmental intervention. Ultimately, polluters argue that government should leave well enough alone and allow nature to take its own course. The obvious rebuttal is that in fact there is very little "natural" left in nature. Man has so altered the physical environment in which he now lives that to argue that government ought not to interfere with "nature" is ludicrous.

Very few residents of the metropolitan areas of the United States, which housed seventy-three percent of the population in 1970, would argue that they are living beside Walden's Pond—nor even within commuting distance. They may think that their present environment is an ideal setting for their lifestyle, but most would agree that it is an artificial setting created largely by man himself. Even the minority of American citizens living in areas remote from urban concentrations are not far removed from evidences of man's conquest of his original environment, whether one is an Appalachian who lives surrounded by the devastation of strip mining or a western sheep rancher who wonders about the connection between the recent reduction of his herd and the nearby army arsenal of biological and chemical weapons. Few Americans live unaffected by man's ability to alter nature or harness the environment to his own desires, nor would the vast majority want to attempt such a life.

There are those who proffer the government's surfeit of activities and the taxpayer's burden as arguments against governmental intervention to preserve what is still natural in the environment. These arguments also do not hold up. Even the most laissez-faire of political theorists agree that a legitimate governmental goal is to provide a stable context within which individual citizens can work out their private fortunes. One of government's traditional goals has been to create, through the necessary use of police and armies, a peaceful social environment in which people may work and play with minimum anxiety about their personal safety. Government also tries to provide a stable economic environment in which citizens may invest and profit with confidence in a sound monetary system and honest fellow traders, who perceive the final threat of court and prison if they do not abide by their contractual agreements.

Efforts to stabilize the physical environment are analogous to these kinds of government activities. History is filled with examples of governments' efforts to control the natural environment, dating from the moment when the first headman convinced his followers to collectively build a levee against the perennial floods of a nearby river. To date, the majority of U.S. government projects affecting the physical environment have been aimed at "improving" on nature for the benefit of man, whether it be the Department of Agriculture's enthusiasm for dumping tons of insecticides and fertilizers on fields to increase crop yield, or the U.S. Army Corps of Engineers' enthusiasm for damming streams for the sake of flood control, irrigation, and the generation of hydroelectricity.

What exactly constitutes an "improvement" is, however, the critical question today. A growing portion of the population contends that it should be the public policy of American government to redress the balance, to put its weight on the side of nature and work to restore the natural state of the physical environment. While the net effect of past governmental activities has been to alter the environment to meet human needs, the government has also undertaken activity on behalf of a more natural setting. A minority of the population have always felt more sinned against than benefitted by their contemporaries' conquest of the air, earth, and water, and has so informed the authorities. Occasionally the minority's point of view has prevailed, and laws, edicts, and other outputs of government have been passed, recognizing the hazard to health and welfare caused by man-made changes to the environment. As early as 1307 in England a royal proclamation was issued prohibiting the burning of coal in furnaces because of the resultant acrid condition in the air above London. Admittedly most such statements of policy have gone unenforced, but at least one unfortunate found that the 1307 English edict was more than symbolic when he was executed for the offense the following year.[2] Although interest in environmental control has increased in the second half of the twentieth century, both in the United States and in other industrial countries, conflict over this issue is not new. A history of environmental policy exists, and in order to comprehend where we are today and where we may be headed tomorrow, it is useful to see where we have been in the past.

## EARLY ENVIRONMENTAL POLICY IN U.S. COURTS

Traditionally there has been a conflict between those persons and groups who wished to use communally held natural resources as sinks (natural dumping grounds for man's wastes) and those who considered themselves injured by such indiscriminate use of the earth, air, and water nearest them. Nevertheless, the same individual could and often did play the first role under one set of circumstances and the second under a different set—typically when his own wastes were less than someone else's. Until recently the arena where this dispute was played out most often was the courts, the traditional arbiter of individual conflicts for society. Property owners who felt injured by others' wastes dumped into the environment near them sued to have law-enforcement officials punish the alleged wrongdoer. In some instances, as in the case of our coal-burning Londoner, a public policy proclaimed pollution to be antisocial behavior. Even when the authorities were not eager to enforce them, laws existed that supported the injured party in his complaint.

In cases where no legislation applied, there were traditional common-law concepts such as that of personal injury to fall back on. In such cases the complaining party asked to be compensated for the damage he had suffered at the hands of the defendant: A farmer who had lost a head of cattle that had drunk from a stream polluted by an upstream municipality's raw sewage might sue to recover the replacement value of his cow. The burden of proof customarily fell on the plaintiff, who had to show after each injury that it was a particular polluter who had wronged him. Given the costs in time, energy, and legal talent required to pursue the argument, only the most stubborn and affluent litigant could afford the price of his tenacity. From the viewpoint of the complainant, the greatest drawback to such judicial remedies was that financial compensation did not relieve his injury. If the court found that the dumping of wastes presented a permanent nuisance, it could simply fine the defendant at a higher rate than the damages for a single cow. The victor discovered that his legal recourse was quickly exhausted, since the polluter paid only once for his continuing activities. This doubtless was the result of many of the court cases that appear at first glance to have constituted a victory for antipollution forces. From the viewpoint of defendants it is still cheaper and no doubt preferable to pay one or even several damage claims than to install pollution-control devices that would permanently eliminate the problem. Both litigants know this fact when they begin any new argument in court, and judges too are well aware that any compensation they may award the plaintiff will not solve his problem, nor those of others who use the same water.[3]

An equity suit—as its name implies—alters a given situation to a fairer one for both parties, unlike the preceding type of lawsuit. The plaintiff does not sue for damages, but applies for a court order enjoining the defendant to change his behavior: A court might issue an injunction decreeing that a polluter either cease dumping wastes into the water flowing by a farmer's property or treat those wastes to a point no longer constituting a danger to an undiscerning cow. In the past, this type of case has proved even more difficult for antipollution forces to win. All the difficulties of proof faced by the plaintiff in damage suits are present here too. In addition, the final and overwhelming weapon of the defense has been that the court needs to "balance the equities" between the two interests. In so doing, legal theorists have developed the doctrine of reasonable use of water by all riparian owners, regardless of the fact that one use may render the water unfit for another kind of use. If the polluter is performing a service for the community, such as disposing of human wastes or manufacturing cement, paper, or steel and in so doing providing employment for part of the population, the courts have normally found that the small damage endured by one farmer is of relatively little economic importance.[4]

It is especially difficult for a court to balance the equities in favor of the antipollution complainant when it is evident that many different polluters have contributed to his injuries. However, when more than one lower-stream user is harmed, it should be possible for fellow sufferers to make a concerted attack against the same source of pollution. Until the 1970s, however, the commonality of their injury was not sufficient to motivate private property owners to band together and create cases demonstrating that their combined losses were greater than the polluters' cumulative benefits to the community. The logistics of developing such arguments and the difficulties of coordination presented major obstacles. The creation of organizations such as the Natural Resources Defense Council and the Environmental Defense Fund, in which environmentally oriented lawyers, scientists, and laymen combine their resources to make their arguments before the courts, has only begun to overcome these obstacles.

The creation of such groups is, however, a very recent development. Throughout the nineteenth century and the first two-thirds of the twentieth, the general tenor of court decisions at all levels indicated that pollution of natural resources was considered a necessary evil when it occurred in conjunction with some more worthwhile acts, such as the production of goods for society. While the courts did not prescribe pollution of natural resources, neither did they proscribe it. As with most other public policies enacted by government, pollution control was not considered totally good nor wholly bad, but was accepted as a matter of degree. Some degrees of pollution were tolerable and others were not, depending on the differences between the costs and benefits produced by them. Due to the relative lack of legislation on the subject, judge-made policy proceeded on an ad hoc basis. While an overall pattern was discernible, individual judges varied in their willingness to accept environmental complaints as legitimate. Private civil law rather than public law provided the main social-control mechanism, thus obscuring patterns of public-policy making from the view of social scientists and the public at large.

## LEGISLATIVE ACTION

It is rare that any question of public policy reaches one arena of government and remains in its exclusive domain. For just as there are winners in each arena, so are there losers, and the latter are unlikely to accept their defeat until they feel they have exhausted all potential remedies. Antipollution forces predictably took their cause beyond the courts and into the legislative and executive branches.

One early example of this procedure at the federal level was the passage in 1890 of the Rivers and Harbors Act, a law designed to regulate obstructions to navigation after the U.S. Supreme Court held that there was no common-law rule for such regulation.[5] The law was amended twice, the last time in 1899. It remains on the statute books today to inform us that the official policy of the U.S. government prohibits industrial-waste discharge into any navigable waterway in the United States without the express permission of the U.S. Army Corps of Engineers. As most Americans interested in the environment are now aware, during the first seventy years of the law's existence it was hardly, if ever, used for pollution-control purposes; at present it seems highly unlikely that it will ever be used for such purposes.[6]

With this exception, during the nineteenth and early twentieth centuries the U.S. Congress was not the forum for discussion of one's grievances concerning pollution control. State and municipal lawmaking bodies, whose police powers over health and welfare gave them broader jurisdiction than the federal government exerted over the environment, were more responsive to environmental concerns. By the turn of the twentieth century most U.S. cities (and especially those that had experienced typhoid epidemics) had public-health ordinances regulating the disposal of human wastes. These statutes emulated the earlier laws of the older, more crowded cities of Europe. The government considered the health hazard created by allowing everyone to run his untreated wastes into the streets or open ditches sufficient justification for coercing private property owners to pay to be connected to the city's sewer system. Nevertheless, privies and septic-tank systems still exist in large cities today. In the development of public policies, administration of the law does not always reflect its intention. However, local health authorities were more concerned with the enforcement of their sewage laws than was the U.S. Army Corps of Engineers with the pollution-control aspects of its Rivers and Harbors Act.

At the same time that cities assumed authority for waterborne wastes, they passed ordinances concerning solid-waste removal.

Often this service remained in private hands, but health authorities asserted control over the deposit sites for the collected debris. As in the case of water-borne sewage their primary aim was to facilitate the removal of unwanted matter to a location which would minimize the threat to the health of their constituency, especially the politically relevant portion that influenced city hall.

At least a portion of the population—allergy sufferers or fastidious housekeepers—was also sensitive to soot particles in the air. Many citizens would be surprised to learn how early their own city government passed a prohibition against open-air burning. As in the case of court decisions, different municipalities treated problems of the environment according to their own scale of importance. Nevertheless, a pattern did emerge whereby local health ordinances proclaimed publicly that pollution should be controlled when it proved a threat to the health of citizens in a limited jurisdiction.

Municipal authorities had little interest in wastes, whether solid, air-borne, or water-borne, once they had been eliminated from the town. It was not long, therefore, before those municipalities and private-property owners downstream or downwind from the outfall pipes and burning dumps of the largest users of shared water and air resources urged the state government to enter the fight. State laws were often eloquently phrased by legislators, who proclaimed that it was the policy of their state to preserve the natural environment. But these laws were underenforced and administered more to the satisfaction of polluters who had greater political influence than to the satisfaction of those who wanted firm government control.

Today the pollution-control argument goes on simultaneously at all three levels of government. Those forces disappointed in the results obtained by local and state laws pin their hopes on federal initiatives in the pollution-control field. This may or may not be realistic, but it is certainly a time-honored tactic among political protagonists for the dissatisfied to broaden the conflict and seek a larger number of participants in the fight against unsatisfactory policy outcomes.

## THE NEW ENVIRONMENTALISM

Writers today often point to public environmental policies as a recent development. Yet some of the population (an admittedly small segment) has long been concerned with the environment although until lately their victories have been rare. We have defined public policy as those things that government decides to do or not do, and must recognize that as long as there is a physical environment there must be some related environmental policy. If the present condition of our earth, air, and water were as degraded as possible because of all the waste produced by the U.S. population, then we could conclude that our government has followed the passive policy of allowing total pollution of the environment to occur.

A close inspection of the waterways and atmosphere near our nation's population centers might lead to this inaccurate conclusion. Nevertheless, there are many sewage-treatment plants in the United States, some in operation for decades, and most cities have now replaced their open smoking dumps with sanitary landfills or closed incinerators. None of these produces a totally clean environment, but all change to some degree the amount of pollution released into the air and water. A degraded physical environment did not suddenly descend upon us in 1960 or 1970: It, like poverty, has been here as long as we have, and some people have been arguing over solutions for just that long.

Until recently, the degraded condition of earth, air, and water in the United States went comparatively unnoticed by much of the population. Public-opinion pollsters have only recently added questions concerning the environment to their questionnaires, but none failed to register a large increase in public interest in the subject from 1965 to 1970. Of those persons surveyed in 1965, for example, only twenty-eight percent perceived air pollution and thirty-five percent perceived water pollution as serious problems; but by 1970 these percentages had increased to sixty-nine percent and seventy-four percent respectively. In a different survey in which people were queried directly about changes they have perceived in their own environment, only three percent reported any improvement whereas over fifty percent felt it had worsened in recent years. When asked whether they would be willing to have government play an increasing role and spend more money on air- and water-pollution control, more than half wanted to expand the federal program, an indication that by the late 1960s a majority of Americans viewed pollution control as a legitimate governmental function. Finally the acid test was reached: Were people willing to pay for an increased program? While more than fifty percent of American taxpayers were willing to have a token tax increase of from \$15 to \$20, the majority resisted the idea of a \$100 increase. The dividing line was drawn at about \$50 in those surveys that explored this sensitive subject of financing.[7]

Proponents of greater control over our artificially created environment increased their support in the late sixties and early seventies throughout the nation but especially among that part of the population now being wooed most ardently by politicians. No poll, whatever its source, fails to reveal that pollution control appeals most to the educated, affluent residents of suburbs. This division in the population's perception of pollution is easily explained by the common notion that the affluent can afford to demand and fund governmental services at a higher level than can the poor. The latter, while they often bear the brunt of the effects of pollution, are too engrossed in obtaining necessities such as employment and food to care much about soot-filled skies and untreated sewage. In the struggle for hard-to-obtain governmental funding, those groups seeking more money for welfare and other social services view environmental control as a competitor.

On the national level, policy analysts who compare spending levels among the several states have noted a definite relationship between pollution-control programs and levels of affluence.[8] A state like California, which has been able to meet more of its residents' basic needs, is willing to spend a larger percentage of its revenues on pollution control than a state like Mississippi, whose spending level is low on all programs. On the international level, too, the stands taken by various countries at the 1972 Stockholm conference on the environment demonstrate this idea. There it was the most highly industrialized and prosperous countries who sought international agreement on pollution-control programs. Poorer nations, more interested in raising their standards of living, argued that it was now their turn to exploit the natural resources that others had been using for so long. Rising expectations with regard to necessities give way to rising expectations with regard to amenities when the opportunity presents itself.

An alternative explanation for the affluent's relative willingness to spend on pollution control is the greater pollution in rich states than in poor ones. This explanation holds whether the states be Mississippi and California or the United States and India, for there is truth in the equation that "affluence = effluents." The demands of the citizenry of different administrative units for pollution control reflect real differences in need. If any proof of this be desired, one need only tour a city on garbage-pickup day and observe the differences between the amounts of trash generated by affluent as opposed to more modest households. Both those persons and nations concerned with squeezing the last ounce of nutritive value from a limited resource base cannot afford waste and thus produce less waste. Western Europe and the United States may be willing to expend more public funds on cleaning up because they indeed have more to clean up. Given such technological innovations as nuclear generating plants and triple packaging, the volume and toxicity of wastes we must dispose of increase at a greater rate than even population. Biologists, chemists, and other natural scientists whose research has uncovered some unexpected effects from environmental pollution have called increased attention to the worsening of our environment. Nevertheless, the damage is there for all to view, and many more are doing so now than have done in the past.

Regardless of how we choose to explain the growth in demand for reduction of pollution within the United States, the question remains: Which side of the controversy will succeed in shaping public policy to meet more of its demands? The number of citizens who perceive greater benefits than costs from cleaning up the environment is growing. However, those who emphasize the cost portion of the equation have usually been more successful. Recently, the energy shortage in the winter of 1973–74, the constantly rising inflation combined with unemployment and a general worsening of economic conditions, and the convulsive end to the second Nixon administration have all drawn public attention away from this new area of concern. In some cases economic factors have helped opponents of pollution control to create a backlash in public opinion against further governmental involvement. Nevertheless, policy makers in all branches and all levels of government have played and will continue to play a role in deciding what happens to our environment in the future. The shape of that future and the impact that public policy in the United States will have on the quality of the average American's environment remain to be seen.

## SUMMARY

The argument that environment control is not a legitimate task of government, and that whatever happens to our earth, air, and water is best left to nature is specious; all human activities alter the physical environment to some degree, either directly or indirectly, and most of them have the passive acquiescence, if not the active support, of government. Traditionally, while there has been no single public policy in the United States for environmental control, different branches of government have evolved and administered many policies at different levels. During the nineteenth and early twentieth centuries the net effect of decisions made by governmental officials produced the policy that pollution is a necessary evil to be endured whenever it is the by-product of some beneficial activity—a notion still current among many citizens and policy makers.

Some individuals remain content with the general policy worked out on a piecemeal basis in the past. The number of those who are not is increasing whether because of a worsening of actual conditions, an increase in expectations concerning the environment, or a combination of the two. If the various branches and levels of government allow individuals to make increasingly unpleasant their own and others' surroundings, then we must recognize this as a conscious choice among alternative options. The remainder of this book explores the kinds of options chosen in the past, their results, and the choices still before us.

## NOTES

1. Thomas R. Dye, *Understanding Public Policy* (Englewood Cliffs, N.J.: Prentice-Hall, 1972), p. 1.
2. Thomas M. Schmitz, "Pollution, Law, Science, and Damage Awards," *Cleveland Law Review* 18 (1969): 456.
3. In the case of City of Harrisonville v. U.S. Dickey Clay Mfg. Co., 289 U.S. 334 (1933), the U.S. Supreme Court admitted that the $500 fine it was upholding was less than the cost of abatement facilities needed to remedy the situation.
4. In 1886, for example, in Pennsylvania Coal Co. v. Sanderson, 113 Pa. 126 (1886), a Pennsylvania court decided that the importance of developing natural resources was more significant than any damage suffered by a lower riparian owner complaining about acid-mine drainage.
5. Willamette Iron Bridge Co. v. Hatch, 125 U.S. 1, 8 (1888) and U.S.C. 407 (1971).
6. See Chapter Five.
7. Hazel Erskin, "The Polls: Pollution and Its Costs," *Public Opinion Quarterly* 36 (Spring 1972): 120–38.
8. Thomas R. Dye, *Politics, Economics, and the Public: Policy Outcomes in the American States* (Chicago: Rand McNally, 1966).

CHAPTER TWO

# Phases of Public Policy

## FORMULATION

One method used by public-policy analysts to explain a frequently complex process is to divide it into several stages or phases of development. The first of these is policy formulation, during which a problem is politicized or brought into the political arena for debate by public-policy making bodies. Whether the arena chosen is the judicial, the legislative, or the executive, and whether at the local, state, or federal level is unimportant. An input from the polity—a demand by an individual citizen or, more commonly, by a group interest asking for governmental funds and/or assistance—generates or renews a discussion in any political arena.

Some demands are directed toward outputs that will benefit only one part of the population, for example, increased subsidies to wheat producers or welfare payments to the poor. More often, however, proponents of a program argue that it will benefit all of society and should be enacted by the government in the "public interest." Rarely does any governmental policy benefit all citizens equally, since some will inevitably derive more pleasure, satisfaction, or pure economic profit from a public policy than will others. Only a foolish group phrases its demands in such a way that it appears to ask for a program designed to benefit itself alone. It is possible to argue that almost any policy provides benefits for the entire public either directly (getting criminal elements off the streets) or indirectly (providing employment for groups that otherwise might become criminal elements).

The general public benefits accruing from environmental-control policies are more evident than are those stemming from many other programs. All individuals are affected by defense spending and by an improved physical environment, and, while all citizens are not equally desirous of being defended against foreign invasion or an unhealthful environment, once the government has decided to provide these amenities it is hard for individuals to avoid their effects.

As indicated in Chapter 1, the appropriate attitude for government to take toward the environment has long provoked periodic debate at various levels and branches of government. Discussion of pollution control has increased in intensity in the United States as well as in other developed countries in recent years. Public policy on pollution has at least reached the stage of formulation, but this phase has not been completed nor is its eventual completion likely. Public-policy formulation is a constant, ongoing process, and one or more public decisions taken on a subject does not forever remove that topic from public debate. Once a particular issue has become politicized both politicians and some part of the public usually maintain a continuing interest in it. In addition the losers in every debate who wish to reactivate the discussion provide a kind of built-in mechanism for the perpetuation of any argument once begun. It is commonly noted that public and private bureaucracies, once established, find it difficult to disband, and this inability reinforces the built-in mechanism. Even when the problems that they were designed to handle have been resolved in some way, bureaus, offices, and interest groups tend to linger on, creating new, related tasks and raising new issues.

One example of this phenomenon is the committee system of the U.S. Congress. When public attention focused on the proper role of the federal government in pollution control, congressional leaders searched for appropriate committees to discuss the numerous proposed environmental bills. One solution was to place a bill in an existing committee that had already developed expertise in the area, for example, the House of Representatives' Committee on Public Works. The Senate, on the other hand, created a new structure, a Subcommittee on Air and Water Pollution. Once the problem of where to send new bills has been settled—sometimes arbitrarily by congressional leaders—the arrangements gather a momentum of their own. Individual congressmen, senators, and their staffs develop their own expertise in these matters; some do so out of a personal conviction, others out of a desire to please a portion of their constituency, and others simply because a question whose "time has come" coincides with their own need to create a new image or change the old.[1] Today there are numerous access points in Congress for groups that wish to make demands for a cleaner environment, and it seems unlikely that the numbers of committees and subcommittees devoted to this topic will be reduced in the near future.

## LEGITIMATION

The second stage of the public-policy process is legitimation of policy. During this period, public-policy outputs (authoritative acts of government) are produced. Such outputs take many different forms, although it is all too easy to equate them with the passage of new laws by Congress or the creation of constitutional amendments. Certainly these are good examples of legitimation, but equally apt examples are administrative decisions made by the Environmental Protection Agency (EPA), executive orders promulgated by the president, municipal ordinances passed by city councils, and court decisions handed down by any level of the judiciary. Simultaneous policy formulation in Congress, the courts, and the executive branch of government, may simultaneously result in different (and sometimes conflicting) policy outputs.

One example of a direction-changing policy output, clearly labeled and legitimated, is the National Environmental Policy Act of 1969, passed by Congress and signed into law by the president on January 1, 1970. The purposes of NEPA were:

> To declare a national policy which will encourage productive and enjoyable harmony between man and his environment; to promote efforts which will prevent or eliminate damage to the environment and biosphere and stimulate the health and welfare of man; to enrich the understanding of the ecological systems and natural resources important to the Nation.[2]

This law clearly symbolizes the dedication of the federal government to a cleaner environment. Today, however, many political analysts question the utility of symbolic policy outputs. Symbols are subject to different interpretations, and it is necessary to discover what the language means in practice, as well as in theory. What, for example, does "productive and enjoyable harmony between man and his environment" mean? Should the emphasis be on "productive"? If so, industrial producers of waste by-products will not be long in arguing that practically any economically productive enterprise is indeed in "harmony" with nature. Other interpreters of the act would argue that they find *no* degree of "harmony" between man and environment "enjoyable" unless the environment is kept free of any of the effects of man's activities. A statement of purpose in a law's preamble has no effect other than to galvanize public opinion to a common cause or inspire potential violators to change their ways voluntarily. Few concrete results arise from hortatory language that urges people to alter their behavior without giving them any further motivation for doing so.

In addition to the problem of interpretation, there is one of sincerity. Some symbols are so valued by the public that it is difficult for governmental decision makers not to invoke them regardless of their personal opinions or intentions. Many governments have proclaimed a policy of peace, on which they dwell stentoriously while preparing actively for war. Some have even had a forcefully worded policy of peace while actually conducting a shooting war, as most people living in the twentieth century are too well aware. For the purposes of this book, therefore, pious declarations of intent do not define public policy, although they sometimes are useful for comparing the stated intention of government with its actual activities. While we shall not ignore the declarations of government, these constitute a logical beginning for a discussion of public policy rather than an ending. Instead of capping our story with the passage of a law, the rendering of an executive order, or a court decision, the legitimation stage is only the opening round in a continuing process.

## IMPLEMENTATION

To progress beyond the rhetoric of public-policy outputs and determine whether or not they produce any tangible results, we reach a third phase of public policy, implementation, which includes the administration or enforcement of laws. Much of what transpires under this heading is actually public-policy formulation and legitimation; frequently high-level decisions are phrased in glittering generalities that have little meaning until they have been interpreted and amended during the implementation stage. Administrative decisions, in the form of agency guidelines, often interpret a vaguely worded law that has been designed to please a variety of interests. Since most environmental policies aim at regulating the behavior of people or organizations (including government agencies), what happens or fails to happen in the implementation stage is the real meaning of public policy for environmental control. It is as correct to speak of a policy of delay and procrastination as one of vigorous enforcement. We must look at the behavior of the regulators—their willingness to hold hearings, render orders, initiate court cases, and do anything else that the law authorizes them to do—before we can determine the nature of a policy. The numbers of court cases initiated and concluded, the subsequent changes in behavior of polluters, represent the real policy direction of government toward the environment more accurately than mere formal statements of the law.

To continue with our legitimation example, the National Environmental Policy Act also contains some less amorphous policy statements than those of the preamble. The most important involves the filing of environmental-impact statements (EISs) by all federal agencies that contemplate any activity "significantly affecting the quality of the human environment." These statements must include:

1. a description of the potential environmental impact
2. any adverse environmental effect that cannot be avoided should the proposal be implemented
3. alternatives to the proposed action
4. discussion of the relationship between local short-term uses of the environment and the maintenance and enhancement of long-term productivity
5. any irreversible commitments of resources involved[3]

Many of the phrases within this section [102 (c)] are obviously also subject to multiple interpretations. For example, how great must the effect be to "significantly affect" the environment? Nevertheless, they do represent a more precise prescription for governmental action than does the preamble. It is now the responsibility of federal agencies who perceive themselves as undertaking actions with significant effects on the environment to alter their behavior.

Most federal agencies have complied with the announced requirement that they file environmental-impact statements. Between the creation of the act and July 1, 1974 the Council on Environmental Quality (CEQ) received draft or final impact statements on 5,474 agency actions, over sixty percent of which have been accepted as final, and the projects they represent are now either under way or completed (see Table I). Decision makers in most federal agencies evidently believe that they must now write impact statements on certain kinds of activities, but many questions remain unanswered by

TABLE I

Environmental Impact Statements Filed With CEQ Through June 1974

| | |
|---|---:|
| Department of Transportation | 2,656 |
| U.S. Army Corps of Engineers | 1,063 |
| Department of Agriculture | 525 |
| Department of Interior | 381 |
| Atomic Energy Commission | 175 |
| Federal Power Commission | 107 |
| General Services Administration | 77 |
| Department of Housing and Urban Development | 84 |
| Department of Defense (except Corps of Engineers) | 87 |
| Environmental Protection Agency | 62 |
| National Aeronautics and Space Administration | 39 |
| All others | 228 |
| Total | 5,474 |

Source: Council on Environmental Quality, *Fifth Annual Report* (Washington, D.C.: U.S. Government Printing Office, 1974): 390.

this simple listing of statements: Have *all* federal agencies perceived their responsibilities in this area to the same extent? Would interested parties such as CEQ members and conservation organizations agree with each agency's decisions as to which projects require impact statements?

What began as a largely voluntary action on the part of most federal agencies has been considerably influenced by public complaint and numerous court decisions, as well as by two different sets of guidelines established by CEQ during the intervening period. It is still usually left up to the discretion of each agency to determine whether or not a particular project it is contemplating warrants an impact statement. The responsibility of the Council on Environment Quality's limited staff extends merely to accepting and filing such statements, *not* to reviewing them, much less infiltrating every other federal agency to determine whether all possible statements have been written. Therefore, we have no notion of what proportion of actions undertaken by the federal government in the first four and a half years of NEPA's implementation these 5,474 reports represent. A literal reading of Section 102 leads to the conclusion that official U.S. policy requires the drafting of environmental-impact statements for all important undertakings. A careful review of the compliance level of the law convinces us, rather, that it is the policy of some agencies to underutilize the act and of others to overutilize it. Which "policy" should be considered the real public policy of the U.S. government? We cannot say at this point, but to consider the wording of the law as the only actual policy that the U.S. government has toward the environment is misleading, to say the least.

## IMPACT

Just as the line between legitimation and implementation is a fine one, the distinction between implementation and the fourth stage—impact—is a difficult one to make. The impact or outcome stage, as the words imply, involves the effects that the policy has on its expressed goal. The first desired result of NEPA was to force potential official disrupters of the environment to consider the possible impact of their projects on the earth, air, and water around them. The framers of the law hoped that if authoritative decision makers inside the federal government wrote down their own perception of how their proposed programs would affect the environment, they would become more sensitive to environmental consequences. Individual conscience is not the only force on which NEPA relies, however. Federal bureaucrats now know that external observers, including state and local agents and the general public, can review CEQ's files to alert themselves to federal intentions. This knowledge may also motivate such decision makers to think more seriously about environmental damage than they might otherwise do.

The logical question to ask concerning this level of impact is: Have any projects been altered because officials in federal or contract agencies spent time drafting impact statements to file with CEQ? In the words of a critic of the program, was there any effect other than "a helluva lot more detailed paperwork?"[4] While the law does allow for comments on the impact statements by other governmental agencies (local, state, as well as other federal agencies, including CEQ) and by private citizens, the ultimate decision—whether to continue with the project as planned, alter it to accommodate the wishes of others, postpone, or scrap the whole thing—rests with the originating agency. The CEQ, in its advisory role to the president, has the potential power to affect such decisions. On rare occasions, CEQ has had sufficient influence with the president to effect an impact on this level, such as in 1970 when President Nixon ordered a halt to the partially completed Cross-Florida barge canal because the favorable environmental-impact statement drafted for it had elicited considerable protest among environmentalists and some politicians. A complete picture of the net effect of such impact statements, however, is possible only after a review of (1) all draft statements, (2) comments by other concerned parties, (3) final statements that followed the comments, and (4) the form in which the projects were carried out.

Ultimately, the impact of all environmental policy must be defined by the physical environment it produces. Although environmental degradation may arouse public opinion and all three phases of the public-policy process may be completed, the actual condition of the environment can continue to deteriorate. This is not proof that the announced public policy has had *no* effect. The old concept of running hard in order to stand still applies especially to the environment; if the public policy of our government were less effective we would be backsliding at an accelerated rate. It is difficult to measure such negative results, much less evaluate them, in terms of the efficiency of other public policies. Most environmental-control measures are still at that stage in their development where scientists argue with each other over the observable effects, and no clear pattern has yet emerged. Without eventually facing this problem of ultimate effectiveness, any discussion of environmental public policy is at best a laboratory exercise with little constructive result to offer the average citizen who is interested in the condition of his or her air, earth, and water.

## FEEDBACK

The last stage in the public-policy process is the feedback loop, when other governmental officials, as well as the public, react to the effects of the policy. Such reactions may be both negative and positive. Interests that originally argued in favor of the policy and feel cheated because they do not observe the anticipated results quickly enough may, therefore, demand stronger measures. At the same time, persons who object to the regulation of their behavior may enlist the support of others who did not initially foresee any restrictions on their freedom of action and undertake to reverse the policy direction. The original authoritative allocation of values is rarely left undisturbed; one policy output, whether symbolic or tangible, is never the end to a complex story but only one chapter in an ongoing saga. The policy formulated yesterday often phrases the question posed to decision makers today.

One of the most common effects of NEPA and the resultant environmental-impact statements has been new demands for authoritative decisions. Such inputs to the political process have come mostly in the form of civil suits over the lack of an environmental-impact statement for a particular governmental project or the inadequacy of the impact statements already filed with CEQ. In the now-famous Alaska-pipeline case, environmentalists obtained a federal-court injunction in 1970 prohibiting the Department of the Interior from issuing a permit for construction of a pipeline over public lands, on the grounds that the potential damage to the fragile tundra and wildlife in Alaska necessitated an environmental impact statement prior to starting construction.[5] After the completion of an impact statement in 1972 and the issuance of the permit on the grounds that public benefits to be derived from the increased oil supply outweighed any potential damage to the environment, other court arguments unrelated to NEPA further delayed groundbreaking. This is a good example of how a decision to alter the environment made by one policy formulator, the Department of the Interior, can be postponed by actions taken by a second authoritative decision-making body, in this case a federal court.

The judiciary is not the only arena in which arguments generated by the interpretation of NEPA are being worked out. After "losing" in the courts the Alyeska Pipeline Service Company, together with Alaskans concerned with the economic benefits to be derived from such a large construction project in their state, took its case to the U.S. Congress. There, in a crisis atmosphere generated by gasoline shortages and under pressure of the oil companies' dire predictions of future fuel scarcity, a bill specifically authorizing the building of the pipeline was passed by a near-unanimous vote in both houses and signed into law on November 16, 1973. In a clear response to earlier court action, and in an attempt to thwart further litigation by environmentalists, the Trans-Alaska Pipeline Authorization Act declared it the will of Congress that:

> The Trans-Alaska Oil pipeline be constructed promptly without further administrative or judicial delay or impediment . . ., and
>
> . . . without further action under the National Environmental Policy Act of 1969.[6]

One policy output—in this case, an act of Congress in 1969—may simply mark the beginning of a new environmental-policy-making process.

## CONCLUSIONS

One method of viewing policy development is linear. Outputs (policy) from one decision-making unit (Congress) are treated as inputs to another (the executive or the court system), and vice versa (see Figure I). An alternative method, and one which more graphically illustrates the method depicted in this book, is circular (see Figure II). There is no discrepancy between the two models but the crucial point to remember is that outputs are not the end of any chain of events. The possibility of reviewing a negative decision—not to construct some environmentally damaging project—always exists. Forces in favor of economic growth and development of natural resources can usually afford to wait until the furor over a particular project dies down and then propose essentially the same project for a different site or change it somewhat, thereby necessitating a repetition of the decisional process. Once environmentalists lose a debate, such as the one over the construction of the pipeline, and the project becomes a reality, there is no hope of their reopening the argument. In this sense a victory for one side is never so final as it is for the other.

FIGURE I
Linear Model of the Public-Policy Process

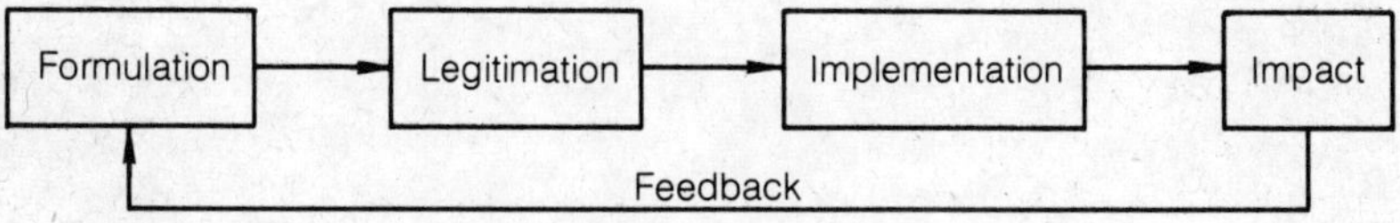

FIGURE II
Continuous Model of the Public Policy Process

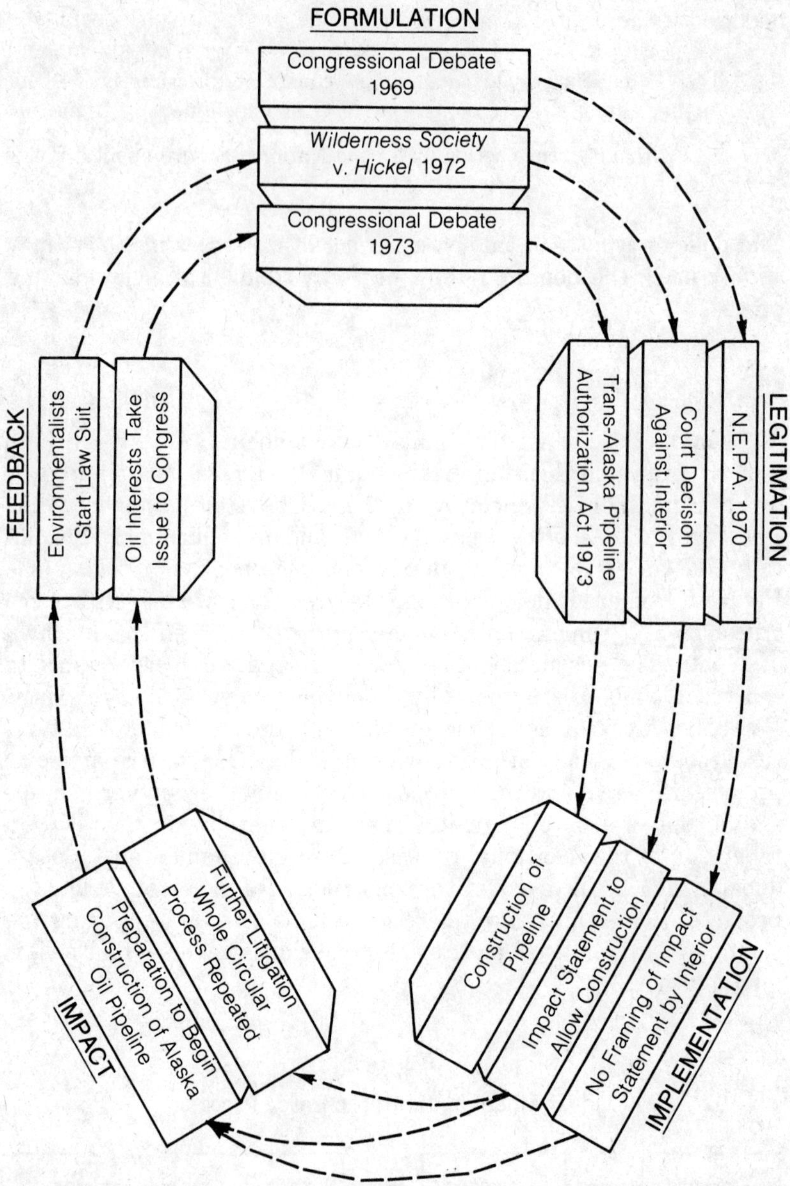

Some policy analysts might view the story of the Alaskan pipeline as evidence that one set of decision makers will revise their opinions about the same problem under changed conditions. Another group of analysts might view the Trans-Alaska Pipeline Authorization Act and the intervening court and administrative decisions as logical steps in working out the meaning of the original legislation and therefore not at variance with the earlier policy statement in NEPA. One conclusion is certain, however: In the years ahead, various interests concerned with environmental matters will continue to use, interpret, and modify NEPA.

The executive branch, including agencies whose task is to prevent environmental degradation, is aware that some environmental-impact statements requested by environmentalists and required by court order may create needless obstruction of some governmental projects. In fact, CEQ itself has issued guidelines indicating that entire categories of governmental action, such as EPA's review of state agencies' determination of water-quality standards, should be categorically accepted and not subjected to individual impact statements. Some of the original congressional framers of NEPA have been sufficiently shocked by its actual use by environmental groups to introduce blanket exemptions to NEPA for their own pet projects involving environmental change. This policy statement has now generated over 400 court cases that, when viewed with the continuing debate in the executive branch and in Congress over the merits of NEPA, demonstrate how one policy output can generate many inputs in the form of demands for interpretation of the government's "real" policy on the environment.

## SUMMARY

Public policy has traditionally been divided into five stages: formulation, legitimation, implementation, impact, and feedback. While these concepts may help us in analyzing and understanding policies, there is considerable overlap in all of them, and people may differ over the place of any given event in the evolution of environmental policy. It is most important, therefore, to view the entire subject as an ongoing process in which decisions made in one level or branch of government influence discussions within other levels or branches as well as within the general populace. The National Environmental Policy Act is one example of a governmental action whose goals are still being worked out. This continuing debate over NEPA is due to both its recent enactment and to unresolved differences of opinion, exhibited by the public and by official decision makers in the United States today, over how to define and attain environmental goals.

## NOTES

1. For a discussion of the roles played by individual congressmen in recent legislative debates, see J. Clarence Davies, III and Barbara S. Davies, *Politics of Pollution*, 2nd ed. (New York: Pegasus, 1974).
2. P.L. 91–190 13th Congress, January 1, 1970.
3. Ibid., Section 102.
4. Comment made by an industrial spokesman to a *National Journal* reporter, quoted in the *National Journal*, September 18, 1971, p. 1932.
5. Wilderness Society v. Hickel, 325 F. Supplement 422 (1970).
6. *New York Times*, November 17, 1973, p. 1.

## BIBLIOGRAPHY: PART 1

Allensworth, Donald T. *The U.S. Government in Action: Public Policy and Change.* Pacific Palisades, Calif.: Goodyear, 1972.

Donovan, John C. *The Policy Makers.* New York: Pegasus, 1970.

Dror, Yehezkel. *Public Policymaking Reexamined.* Scranton, Pa.: Chandler, 1968.

Dye, Thomas R. *Politics in States and Communities.* Englewood Cliffs, N.J.: Prentice-Hall, 1969

———. *Politics, Economics and the Public: Policy Outcomes in the American States.* Chicago: Rand McNally, 1966.

Easton, David: *A Systems Analysis of Political Life.* New York: John Wiley & Sons, 1965.

———. *A Framework for Political Analysis.* Englewood Cliffs, N.J.: Prentice-Hall, 1965.

Edelman, Murray. *The Symbolic Uses of Politics.* Urbana: Univ. of Illinois Press, 1964.

———. *Politics as Symbolic Action.* Chicago: Markham, 1971.

Haveman, Robert, and Margolis, Julius, eds. *Public Expenditure and Policy Analysis.* Chicago: Markham, 1970.

Hofferbert, Richard. *The Study of Public Policy.* New York: Bobbs-Merrill, 1974.

Jones, Charles O. *An Introduction to the Study of Public Policy.* Belmont, Calif.: Wadsworth, 1970

Lasswell, Harold. *Who Gets What, When, and How.* Magnolia, Mass.: Peter Smith, 1950.

Lindblom, Charles E. *The Policy-Making Process.* Englewood Cliffs, N.J.: Prentice-Hall, 1968.

Mitchell, Joyce M., and Mitchell, William C. *Political Analysis and Public Policy.* Chicago: Rand McNally, 1969.

Mitchell, William C. *Public Choice in America.* Chicago: Markham, 1971.

Monsen, R. Joseph, Jr., and Cannon, Mark W. *The Makers of Public Policy: American Power Groups and Their Ideologies.* New York: McGraw-Hill, 1965.

Sharkansky, Ira. *Spending in the American States.* Chicago: Rand McNally, 1968.

———. ed. *Policy Analysis in Political Science.* Chicago: Markham, 1970.

Wade, Larry L. *The Elements of Public Policy.* Columbus, Ohio: Charles E. Merrill, 1972.

Wade, Larry L. and Curry, R. L., Jr. *A Logic of Public Policy.* Belmont, Calif.: Wadsworth, 1970.

Woll, Peter. *Public Policy.* Cambridge, Mass.: Winthrop, 1974.

PART 2

# Environmental Policy Today

CHAPTER THREE

# The Three Faces of Pollution

## THE INTERDEPENDENCE OF ALL POLLUTION

Analogous to policy phases which resist separation into distinct entities, environmental problems are frequently so closely interrelated that a solution for one often creates a new problem elsewhere. Burning solid waste sends particulate matter into the air, where some of it may lodge in the lungs of anyone unlucky enough to inhale at the time. Most of this matter returns to the soil in the form of fallout and eventually finds its way into the waterways of our nation, either through runoff into lakes or streams or seepage into the water table beneath the earth's surface. People residing near a stinking river that is decomposing its organic load anaerobically (without oxygen) will probably identify it as an air-pollution problem first.

An individual faced with a particular disposal problem may choose one of three immediate solutions: bury the material, throw it into the nearest lake, river, or ocean, or burn it, in which case gases and particulate matter will be released into the atmosphere. He may theoretically base his choice on the value he places on each of the three available sinks: land, water, and air. Different cultures regard these three substances as having different values and commanding different degrees of respect. Zoroastrians so revere all three substances that they do not consign dead bodies to any of them but expose the corpses for vultures to consume, as did some native American tribes. Such esoteric matters as the relative sanctity of earth, water, and air are unlikely to enter the calculations of technology-prone American policy makers. Our present value system, the monetary cost of disposal, usually dictates our decisions about where to dispose of unwanted materials.

Even when society chooses to treat wastes to some degree, the problem of ultimate disposal remains. In the case of sewage treatment, regardless of the degree of purity achieved the plant is left with both a liquid waste (effluent) and a solid residue (sludge). It may dispose of the effluent by dumping it into the nearest liquid sink (river, ocean, or lake) or by spraying it onto a land surface (golf course or infertile soil to be readied for growing crops). Many municipal authorities' decisions will depend on their geographical location. (City engineers in Honolulu would certainly use the ocean more often than those in Kansas City.) They may also take the sludge and bury it or burn it. Or, they may tow it out to sea as the cities in the New York coastal areas have done for so many years, resulting in a dead segment of the Atlantic Ocean originally some miles from shore but now rapidly washing back toward the beaches.

Both governmental and private institutions have always dealt separately with the three problems of land, water, and air pollution regardless of their interdependence. The administrative trend today is admittedly toward a wholistic approach in which superagencies such as the national Environmental Protection Agency (EPA) undertake to control all three types of waste. This has not been the practice in the past, nor is it the practice everywhere today. Even within the superagencies themselves there is a division of labor that follows the traditional approach of individually treating land-, air-, and water-pollution problems. Experts who formerly worked in a smaller agency concerned with one aspect of the total picture continue to utilize their special knowledge to deal primarily with water or air pollution or solid-waste disposal, notwithstanding the size of the organization that pays their salary today. This book deals with current policy, with how our decision makers are now attempting to deal with these pollution problems. We must understand the nature of the problem for each resource and the effect of past governmental action, before we can predict the future.

## WATER POLLUTION: THE NATURE OF THE PROBLEM

Water pollution is an eternal dilemma. It is a relative problem without a specific historical beginning. Technically, pollution is the addition to water of substances other than pure $H_2O$, which itself exists nowhere in nature until man has distilled it. Even the purest rainwater collects some impurities as it descends through an impure atmosphere to the earth; for air pollution, like water pollution, is also omnipresent. The realization that pollution must be measured by a continuum should not blind us to the fact that it exists. The larger the waste load placed in a limited water supply the more degraded it becomes, unless man chooses to intervene.

One characteristic of water in its natural state that has made it so attractive as a dumping ground for effluents is the ability of certain bacteria that water normally contains to break down organic wastes into their constituent chemical parts. This capacity of water to decompose biodegradable wastes has led to the concept of its assimilative capacity. The supply of dissolved oxygen in water is also important in the decomposition process, for oxygen is used up during the decomposition of organic matter. When little or no oxygen remains, decay becomes anaerobic and the offensive odor associated with sewage disposal assails the passer-by. Besides causing an objectionable smell, heavy organic waste loads also lead to eutrophication (rapid aging) of water bodies. Oxygen-consuming organisms drive out oxygen-producing ones until an entire lake is filled with decaying organic waste. Most concentrated biodegradable waste can still be successfully eliminated given sufficient time and volume of water and oxygen to complete the job, and this explains the complacent attitude toward the need for treating organic wastes before "final" disposal into the natural-treatment facility. In many watercourses of the United States, however, no waste load is ever fully assimilated before the next slug of organic waste arrives, neutralizing any earlier degree of purity achieved.

An additional pollutant often associated with organic waste is the one best known to both policy makers and the average individual: infectious bacteria, viruses, and other microorganisms that transmit disease. The wastes of diseased individuals entering a common water supply can spread typhoid and other waterborne germs. Fear of such epidemics led to the first efforts to treat effluents by killing such pathogens. If the organisms that decompose organic wastes are to be preserved, there are obvious problems involved with massive disinfection of waterways. Even if our supply of chlorine were sufficiently plentiful and cheap, it is unlikely that we would prefer to reduce all our waterways to swimming-pool sterility.

Two other types of water pollution that human activities have greatly augmented complicate the process of decomposing organic wastes: siltation and temperature changes. The presence of suspended solids reduces the amount of light that can penetrate a body of water and aid plant life in the manufacture of oxygen from carbon dioxide. Increases in water temperature cause the available dissolved oxygen to combine with organic waste at a more rapid rate, thus speeding up the decomposition of biodegradable waste but reducing the amount of oxygen available for oxidizing the next load of organic waste. Both siltation (which builds up sediment in streams and lake beds) and temperature changes have other detrimental effects, such as the elimination of certain aquatic species whose natural habitats may be so altered as to drive them out of an area or eliminate them entirely.

More complicated than organic wastes are inorganic wastes—synthetic organic chemical and mineral substances that cannot be biologically broken down. Many of these are toxic to aquatic life and to many land-dwelling species, including man, if ingested in sufficient quantities either through direct contact with the water or via the food chain. Many of these substances can combine (for better or worse) with other chemicals they meet in lakes and rivers, but the greatest effect that releasing them into waterways has is to distribute them more widely around the country. This distribution may have the desired effect of reducing a given poison's toxicity through reducing its concentration but it is clearly limited by the total volume of water available.

Experts disagree about the level at which various chemical components become dangerous to the health of humans and other animals. Aside from such recognizably immediate dangers as that demonstrated by mercury contamination of fish in 1971, there is the unsolved problem of cumulative long-term, low-level exposure to substances that may become poisonous at an undetermined threshold. In addition to exposure problems, nonbiodegradable artificial matter may also interact with organic wastes in water to complicate eutrophication problems. Plant nutrients, such as the well-known phosphates from detergents, promote the growth of such aquatic flora as algae. Algae, in their decomposed stage, add to the organic waste load on the water's oxygen supply, which in turn accelerates the eutrophication process.[1]

## SOURCES OF WATER POLLUTION

Despite the fact that one source is often associated with a particular type of pollutant (for example, electricity-generating plants associated with increases in water temperature), the problem of regulation is complicated by the fact that there are many different sources for the same type of waste. Most of the wastes previously mentioned existed in nature before man's arrival, but all have been greatly increased because of human activities. Without homo sapiens, natural processes—oxidation of organic wastes and natural dissipation of the more durable toxic chemical elements—served to keep pollution below the danger level. But the ever-increasing human population combined with its by-product, industrial production, have added numerous sources of all these pollutants to those nature has provided.

The type of pollution most commonly and effectively treated is domestic sewage, a primary source of pathogens and organic substances as well as numerous household chemicals (including the well-known phosphate detergents) that resist normal secondary treatment. In 1968, after an extensive inventory of U.S. municipal waste-treatment facilities, it was estimated that the equivalent of the raw wastes from approximately 54,323,000 people was being discharged daily into U.S. watercourses by municipal sewers.[2] This figure does not represent the whole sewage problem, however, for it excludes those persons not connected to any kind of collective sewage system who use individual septic-tank systems or deposit their wastes directly into the water supply or onto land—a good twenty-five percent of the U.S. population.

Much less is known about industrial wastes, since a complete independent inventory of industrial effluents has never been made in this country. Estimates based on the average waste output from different types of industry tested by governmental agencies and on estimates of the amount of production by each type of industry lead to a conservative conclusion that industry contributes considerably more than twice as much organic matter to our water supply as does domestic sewage. In addition to the organic wastes produced by industry there are the more exotic nonbiodegradable wastes that present an even larger problem. Some industrial effluents are in fact processed by local waste-treatment plants, which may be fairly efficient at reducing organic loads but are almost without effect on pollutants that resist treatment and simply run through the system without change.

In addition to domestic and industrial wastes, there are a number of other sources of pollution about which even less is known; consequently, fewer attempts at control have been made. One such source is agriculture, which produces a variety of pollutants. The most obvious kind is animal excrement that becomes concentrated at the feedlot pens where livestock are kept in close confinement prior to slaughter. Some effort is now being made to treat these wastes, but in the past they were washed directly into the nearest stream. Today, as formerly, many organic wastes return to the ecological system through their use as fertilizers for field crops. Most farmers also supplement their animals' natural fertilizing capacity with chemical fertilizers, which, if they are overapplied to or underutilized by crops, will wash off into watercourses. A portion of the insecticides sprayed onto crops for pest control likewise finds its way into the waterways. Besides chemical additives, the soil itself that is washed away during the preparation of the earth for crops contributes to the natural siltation problem of most waterways. Another source of pollution, the practice of irrigating crops (especially in the western United States), increases the mineral (salt) content of the water table by leaching out salts from the soil.

Numerous other sources of wastes, such as run-off from streets, garbage dumps, construction sites, and whatever is placed on the banks of a river or lake, cannot be pinpointed. Vaguely defined sources of pollution (non-point sources) are much less controllable than are identifiable water users who have laid pipes to the nearest stream with the obvious intention of waste disposal. In addition to being almost uncontrollable themselves, non-point sources of pollution add to the burden of the average pollution-control administrator by giving identifiable polluters an excuse for doing nothing about their own effluents.

Since the relative degradation of a body of water is due to the accumulation of wastes, including natural wastes, it is difficult to pinpoint specific guilt for a particular condition. Those polluters who are cited for their contributions are quick to argue that the flotsam and jetsam in the stream from the nearest empty lot, passing boat, picnic or construction site, garbage dump or city street are as offensive as their own effluents. Since most people consider the waterway a public resource equally available to everyone, the identifiable polluter argues that he has as much right to pollute as has the non-point source.

This argument contains some truth. Given that the waterway has a limited assimilative capacity, the identifiable polluter assumes a larger share of the burden for keeping the waterway in acceptable condition than does the non-point source, which assumes nothing. Water pollution is cumulative as well as relative. Responsibility for water pollution penetrates the entire community. Any downstream water user who wants to obtain damages or any water pollution-control administrator carries the burden of demonstrating not only that pollution itself exists but also that the alleged malefactor is indeed the one to blame for a significant portion of that pollution. At times this task has proven insuperable.

## AIR POLLUTION: THE NATURE OF THE PROBLEM

If water pollution seems complicated because of the variety of its sources, consider the task of the air-pollution controller whose problems include not only every factory smokestack and individual building with a heating plant (whether residential or commercial), but also every moving vehicle powered by the internal-combustion engine, each smoldering municipal dump, and every backyard incinerator. Air pollution, like water pollution, is also a cumulative and relative phenomenon with no specific historical beginning or probable end. Man's presence on earth has greatly contributed to the problem, but it has been an incremental process and not an overnight occurrence. It is as difficult to attach blame for a particularly murky sky as for a stinking river. Specific areas such as Los Angeles have special natural problems; in these areas the same amount of man-made pollutants that would constitute only a passing problem elsewhere will have dire consequences if left uncontrolled.[3]

Air, like water, provides a medium in which chemical reactions take place. Some of these promote a cleansing effect and render certain harmful constituents less dangerous. Others combine substances that by themselves would not constitute a threat to human health into extremely deleterious compounds. Air does not, however, share with water its considerable capacity for decomposing organic wastes through bacterial action. Once contaminants enter the atmosphere their reduction is primarily dependent on their natural dispersal through air movements. Their disposal is inevitably into either the soil or water by way of fallout or precipitation.

Although air pollutants are varied and numerous, five main types constitute most of the volume of air pollution, and attempts at control have primarily been directed toward these substances. Carbon dioxide and carbon monoxide together constitute the largest volume of any chemical compound emitted into the air by human activities. Carbon dioxide results from the oxidation of organic fuels. It has no harmful effect on animal life by itself, but the balance between the amount of carbon dioxide and oxygen in the atmosphere is precarious, dependent on the volume of oxygen-producing and oxygen-consuming activities taking place on the earth. Although experts differ on the likely result, they agree that humans have increased the concentration of carbon dioxide over the years. Some experts feel that a continuation of this trend could result in a substantial alteration of the global climate. Carbon monoxide, unlike carbon dioxide, results from the incomplete combustion of organic fuels and is undeniably hazardous to human beings at even low concentrations over extended periods of time. The policy of allowing New York City tunnel-traffic policemen periodic oxygen breaks in the course of their day's work is one recognition of this danger.

Sulfur oxides, a second type of air pollutant, are a group of gases more poisonous to mankind than the same concentration of carbon monoxide. They are produced from the combustion of fuels containing sulfur, primarily coal and oil. There are at least three different approaches to controlling the amount of sulfur oxides in the air: utilizing low-sulfur fuel, removing sulfur from the fuel before combustion, or removing sulfur oxides from the combustion gases.

Hydrocarbons, like carbon monoxide, result from incompletely burned fuels and are produced in about the same quantity as sulfur oxides. They are not so toxic to man in their normal state as either sulfur oxides or carbon monoxide, but in the presence of sunlight they combine with nitrogen oxides to form photochemical oxidants, major constituents of the smog whose irritating properties are well known to most residents of such cities as Los Angeles, Mexico City, and Tokyo.

Nitrogen oxides, the other major compound in photochemical oxidants besides hydrocarbons, are formed when nitrogen combines with oxygen at very high temperatures. Although originally they counted for a relatively small percentage of automobile emissions, an increase in nitrogen oxides is the unfortunate by-product of certain types of emission controls used to reduce hydrocarbons and carbon monoxide. First attempts to control automobile emissions sometimes resulted in increases in air-pollution levels.

The fifth type of air pollutant, particulate matter, of which just plain dirt and soot comprise a large proportion, creates a nuisance as well as a distinct health hazard in most cities. Practically any kind of human activity that pulverizes solid matter contributes some dust to the atmosphere, and now suspended in the air we breathe are such undesirable inhalants as beryllium, asbestos, and lead. Fortunately for those individuals, such as airline pilots, who need good visibility for their work or play, these particles do not remain suspended in the atmosphere. Suspended particles have a natural tendency to adhere together until they weigh enough for gravity to pull them to earth.

## SOURCES OF AIR POLLUTION AND ITS TREATMENT

The sources of air pollution are either moving or stationary. Moving sources are primarily forms of transportation: airplanes, trains, buses, trucks, and the most grievous offender (because of its numbers), the passenger car. About two-thirds of all carbon monoxide, over half of all hydrocarbons, and nearly forty percent of nitrogen oxides produced in the United States are directly attributable to the gasoline-fueled internal-combustion engine. Stationary sources are industrial processes, solid-waste disposal, forest fires, and fuel combustion, both for heating private homes, public buildings, and industries and for creating electric power in generating plants.

where it falls until it decomposes (as in the case of animal manure on farms) or is buried through natural processes. When cattle roamed the open range, this may have been a fine solution. When they are crowded together in feedlots where their wastes accumulate so rapidly that there is little possibility for their absorption into the soil, the problem becomes unwieldy. The density factor applies also to people, whose junk may be unsightly but not a significant problem when dispersed across the landscape. In populous areas the natural-decay solution is undesirable both from an aesthetic as well as a public-health point of view, and consequently local governments in all regions of the country have taken some action. At first the solution was simply to take the debris far enough out of town to remove it from the sight and smell of its original producers. Even today the open dump is the solution for most communities and constitutes the final resting place for the majority of collected solid wastes in the United States.

In areas where land is so valuable that it is impracticable to consign large areas to holding heaps of garbage and to creating buffer zones between those offensive mounds and the population, another solution must be found. One possible answer is the municipal incinerator, which greatly reduces the volume of waste. But this process, too, leaves a solid residue, composed primarily of metals, glass, and plastics, that must finally be disposed of in the earth. The majority of incinerators creates an even more unfortunate by-product—air pollution, because of the incomplete oxidation of combustible matter and the melting of such nonburnables as plastics. The cost of installing electrostatic precipitators to reduce air pollution from incinerators has kept the municipal incinerators a poor third among methods for handling solid wastes.

Many city policy makers have returned to using increasingly scarce land resources for all their solid-disposal needs, but the open dump has frequently been rejected in favor of the sanitary landfill, which is rapidly replacing the dump even in communities that have never invested in any type of incinerator. The major difference between the two methods of land disposal is the practice of covering each day's garbage in the sanitary landfill with a layer of soil sufficiently deep to discourage the local rodent and other pest populations and to eliminate the sight and smell of open dumps. Most sanitary landfills are also planned with another worthwhile goal in mind. The site selected is often a cavity (either man-made, such as a played-out quarry, or a natural canyon) that is filled to the level of the surrounding terrain thus forming a foundation to build on. If the topography is flat, the fill may be used to produce artificial hills for toboggan or ski runs or other recreational purposes.

## LAND DISPOSAL: CONTINUING PROBLEMS

In both landfills and old-fashioned dumps burial in the earth is the ultimate solution to the disposal problem, but burial itself, no matter how rapid, leads to two related problems. The first obvious problem is that land disposal (even by the use of sanitary landfills) is not really a final solution for many kinds of waste. Certain constituents of solid wastes can contaminate the soil, just as they can air and water, when deposited there. The organic waste that is a significant portion of household garbage is one such constituent. Eventually organic matter will decay in the earth, creating more fertile soil but also considerable odor and health hazards. Disease-spreading germs may seep or run off into water supplies regardless of whether the garbage is covered with a layer of soil. Frequently, dumps have been deliberately located in wetland areas—marshes, bays, and other places where land meets water—because of the clear potential for "reclaiming" land by simply filling in the part of the body of water closest to land. Present-day shorelines of many cities from Cleveland to San Francisco are built on the trash of past decades. One goal of sanitary landfills—to choose disposal areas based on potential future use of the areas after filling—is thereby achieved, but it may contradict other goals. Heaps of wet garbage oozing partially decayed organic matter add to the waste loads on waterways receiving the runoff and thereby contribute to the problems associated with using such surface water for water supplies and/or recreational purposes.

Solid waste, besides its organic constituents, also contains all the chemical compounds already detailed under water pollution. Burying hazardous and toxic substances keeps them from passing directly into the water supply, but they will probably find their way into the water table unless biological and/or chemical reactions in the soil render them harmless on their way to that water supply. The simple septic tank relies on this principle of natural assimilation to break down organic wastes before they reach the water table and is therefore located downhill from the household's well. The soil has some capacity for the absorption and alteration of polluting elements, but there is no fundamental difference between burying dangerous substances and dumping them into water once the absorptive capacity of the earth or water has been exhausted.

Burial is still considered the ultimate solution for some wastes most hazardous to human health. Certain precautions have been devised to isolate radioactive wastes and highly toxic chemicals from the surrounding water tables and to prevent them from percolating back to the surface at some later date: lining the burial vault with some supposedly impermeable substance such as steel or concrete, or sinking tanks into the earth. The obvious and important questions are then: When will the containers start to leak? How safe *are* the tanks? It has already happened that highly toxic compounds produced for chemical warfare have corroded their containers and leaked into the surrounding environment.

Burial vaults may create other less predictable risks than spills. In one instance, earthquakes followed the pumping of chemical wastes from the Rocky Mountain Arsenal into a 12,000-foot artificial well near Denver. We have no way of predicting all the destructive effects of the disposal of highly dangerous, long-lived poisons in the earth; nevertheless, the proliferation of deep shafts filled with radioactive and toxic substances is not a reassuring thought for many scientists or laymen. Some would prefer to place the steel-lined vaults in the oceans, a solution that does not resolve any of the difficulties but simply locates them farther from population centers and forces other nations to share the risk with the industrialized producers of such wastes.

A second problem connected with the burial of solid wastes in the earth is the availability of space. Since land is finite there is a limit to the number of canyons and empty quarries that can be filled with the debris of our affluent society. There is even a limit to flatlands accessible to metropolitan areas, where demand exists for garbage hills for future recreation. It is becoming progressively more expensive for urban and suburban sanitation services to transport their collected wastes greater distances for final disposal. In addition to economic constraints imposed by the costs of hauling and purchasing space, increasing political difficulties complicate locating appropriate sites. Are there citizens anywhere who would not object to the use of their community as the repository for someone else's garbage? As settlement becomes denser in outlying areas and governmental units become more concerned with finding sufficient space for their own constituents' use, the search for new garbage sites to replace those already filled becomes more and more competitive.

The difficulty of locating areas that have little value other than for landfill is only one aspect to a much larger problem—that of determining what is the most appropriate use for any parcel of land. Until recently the distribution of available space for various purposes, whether for residency, farming, mining, industry, commerce, transportation, recreation, or even garbage disposal, has been based on the ability of various competitors to pay for available space. Opinion varies radically on the relative value to society of any of these purposes. To some people, a grid housing pattern on one-eighth-acre lots is a fine solution to the problem of providing decent housing for those who need it most. For others, it is simply eye pollution or land pollution with greater impact than any garbage dump. For some, strip mining provides a more economic and less dangerous solution to fuel shortages than deep mining, with a seemingly infinite (if inconveniently placed) potential for landfill. For others, the resultant alteration in landscape, soil erosion, destruction of vegetation, acid drainage into streams, and threat of landslides from piles of mining wastes completely destroy any benefits to be derived from mining.

Alternative solutions to some of these problems, such as reclaiming strip-mined lands, have not been much used in the past. Recent attempts at ameliorative measures, strip-mining legislation aimed at forcing mining companies to clean up after themselves, passed the Congress both in 1974 and 1975, but were successfully vetoed by President Ford each time. Unless there is a considerable shift in political influence in Washington, these kinds of measures are less likely to determine the kind of environment that future generations of Americans will face than will decisions concerning land use that policy makers at all levels of government are now making. The possibility of a national land-use policy seems to remain at some distance in the future, but in order to predict the stages and forms through which it may pass, it is important that we begin by exploring the types of governmental policies dealing with all three aspects of pollution that have been developed up to the present.

## SUMMARY

Water, air, and land pollution are all interrelated, relative, and cumulative phenomena. Each resource has some absorptive capacity for wastes. The relative degree of degradation permissible for each is a function of the eye of the beholder, but there are certain chemical components in all wastes deposited in all three resources that are highly detrimental to human health both in the long and the short run. These chemical pollutants are derived from a variety of sources, including residential, industrial, mining, and agricultural. The problem of finding objective criteria for defining pollution adds to the difficulty of assessing blame for producing the kinds of conditions that everyone complains of at some time. Pollution in this country has grown to a crucial point at which the government must take some positive steps for its abatement. The remainder of the book deals with such policy decisions of government.

## NOTES

1. For a complete description of the composition and properties of water, see Peter Briggs, *Water, the Vital Essence* (New York: Harper & Row, 1967). For a history of the use of water as a waste-disposal system, see Earl Finbar Murphy, *Water Purity* (Madison: Univ. of Wisconsin Press, 1961), Ch. 1. For a discussion of technical problems involved in measuring degrees of pollution, see Louis Klein, *Aspects of River Pollution* (London: Butterworths, 1966). vol. 1.

2. U.S. Department of the Interior, Federal Water Pollution Control Administration, *Inventory of Municipal Waste Facilities in the United States* (Washington, D.C.: U.S. Government Printing Office, 1968).

3. Two sources for a general discussion of the problems of air pollution are Donald E. Carr, *The Breath of Life* (New York: Berkley Medallion Books, 1971); and Louis J. Battan, *The Unclean Sky* (Garden City, N.Y.: Anchor Books, 1971). For technical information concerning both air and water pollution, the best sources are the Council on Environmental Quality's *Annual Reports* (Washington, D.C.: U.S. Government Printing Office), starting in 1970 and extending to the present.

4. There are fewer comprehensive works dealing exclusively with solid wastes rather than with air and water pollution. One exception is William Small, *Third Pollution: The National Problem of Solid Waste Disposal* (New York: Praeger, 1971). The topic, is, however, covered in most readings on pollution, for example, in Garrett DeBell, *The Environmental Handbook* (New York: Ballantine Books, 1970). For up-to-date technical information, the best source is again CEQ's *Annual Reports*. See above, n. 3.

CHAPTER FOUR

# Pollution Control: A State and Local Matter

## LAND-POLLUTION POLICY: AN EMERGING CONCEPT

Opposing groups in every community, including elected and appointed officials, differ concerning the best uses for their limited land resources but most have given the problem little direct attention until recently. There is no basis, however, for saying that there is no governmental policy for land use. Even if there is no comprehensive plan for allocating available land space, decisions made by governmental agencies in the past have greatly influenced existing land-use patterns in the United States today.

Zoning regulations and property-tax rates, based primarily on type of use to which land is put, have been crucial in determining land-use patterns in the United States. For example, the need felt by municipal and county units to raise their tax base by increasing the relative amount of space devoted to residential, commercial, and especially industrial properties has contributed significantly to the reduction in farm acreage nearest our largest population centers. Officials do not advocate any conscious policy to decrease the supply or increase the cost of foodstuffs for their constituents; nevertheless, the result has been to create alarm among scientists concerned over limited supplies of food in the world, who warn about the loss of fertile land simply because of its location near the high-rent district.[1]

On the other hand, in response to the demands of constituents in some localities, such as Westchester County, New York, local governments have utilized existing zoning laws to protect residential areas from incursions from industry, commerce, and, in some wealthy areas, from lower-income housing. Conflicting values and needs have sometimes produced compromise solutions and ambiguous land-use policies in other areas. It is not easy to generalize about how decisions over land use are reached. Most of the conflicts have been resolved at the local level, producing a patchwork-quilt pattern.

Most zoning and tax decisions have been made on an ad hoc basis, often in a crisis atmosphere. Long-range goals and needs best discussed in the context of comprehensive planning have been largely ignored. Today this situation is changing. One of the major concerns of many American cities and towns, whether large or small, new or old, growing or shrinking, is the direction in which they should be moving both in the immediate and distant future. The issues are not new, but today there is a more self-conscious effort to arrive at longer lasting solutions. Planning may produce outcomes no different from the ad hoc patterns of the past, but one by-product of deliberately determined land uses may be greater visibility for these decisions. Citizens within each community are now coming to realize that the condition of their environment is not and does not have to be left to chance.

Today, efforts at planned land use remain at the local level. Piecemeal plans create obvious problems for large areas. If each township competes with its neighbors for increased revenues from areas zoned at the highest tax rates, who will provide land for less profitable but equally necessary recreation facilities and open space? Some states—most notably Delaware, Florida, Maine, New York, and Vermont—have initiated some form of statewide land-use planning in order to cope with such questions. Such efforts still leave untouched the need for interstate cooperation in multistate, metropolitan areas.

On the federal level, public debate over the solution to problems of land use has only begun. We are in the midst of the policy-formulation stage, a phase that air- and water-pollution control occupied twenty to thirty years ago, and attempts at defining land pollution are only now being made. A consideration of the relative benefits to society represented by various uses of the land and different approaches for achieving these goals are still necessary. In 1974 a Land Use Planning Act failed to pass the U.S. House of Representatives, primarily because of the combined opposition of the U.S. Chamber of Commerce and the building trade unions, who viewed the bill as a direct threat to their power and livelihoods.[2] The bill's defeat was partly a casualty of impeachment politics—the result of a conservative backlash of the Nixon administration in its last weeks. The debate is certain to be revived in Congress as well as in the executive branch.

In July 1974, EPA *did* create a modest new division to begin thinking about land-use problems that contribute to air- and water-pollution problems.[3] This division is destined for growth, since it is difficult to think of any pollution that land use does not affect. For example, one major contributing factor to urban air pollution is the number of automobiles in a given city on a given day. This number is largely dependent on the attractiveness and cost of automobile commuting—the relative price of parking, tollways, and public transportation—and the determination of such costs is intimately tied to allocation of land space in metropolitan areas.

The discussion about land-use planning will continue at the national level until the eventual passage of some type of legislation. The aborted bill of 1974 would have left the primary responsibility for land-use planning to local government. Its major change would have been to encourage states, through the utilization of federal grants for planning, to assume control of important land-use decisions like the location of airports and oil refineries and construction in such important areas as wetlands. Some states have already gone further in assuming general planning authority for their jurisdictions, but this federal law would have encouraged *all* states, even the most reluctant, to assume some responsibility for land use.

These initial efforts at national land-use policy formation and the kind of approach originally taken at the national level for both air and water pollution present an interesting parallel. As a result of federal legislation, there has been considerable policy development with regard to air and water on both state and local levels. In order to get some feel for what may happen to land-use planning in the future, it is necessary to turn to those areas—water- and air-pollution control—where considerable policy formulation and implementation have already occurred.

## EARLY REGULATION OF AIR AND WATER POLLUTION

Given the size of the North American continent and the scattered location of its early sparse population, interest in environmental problems naturally arose first at the local level. Motivated by self-interest to combat health and safety hazards, city administrators since the nineteenth century have constructed city sewers and hauled garbage out of town. Besides providing such basic services, however, many city fathers also saw the need to regulate private individuals' behavior if these services were to have the desired effect. Municipal ordinances prohibited open-air burning of garbage within city limits. Building codes stipulated the installation of toilet facilities connected to city sewer lines inside all buildings of a certain size and occupancy.

Today these regulations seem eminently sensible to most urban dwellers, but the battle is far from won. It reasserts itself often in disputes between health officials and suburban real-estate developers. The former often have less confidence than the latter in the capacity of the soil and water table for accepting septic-tank effluents and urge builders to tie into publicly owned sewer lines and treatment plants. Developers are not the only ones to view sewage treatment as a needless expense, however. In the often-confused and overlapping jurisdictions of towns, townships, and counties in suburban areas, local authorities are often reluctant to provide the needed facilities. In 1971, for example, there was a court-imposed moratorium on further residential expansion in Montgomery County, Maryland, outside Washington, D.C., because of the lack of sufficient sewage-treatment capacity for the ever-increasing population.

By the end of the nineteenth century, it had become clear that local, ad hoc methods of handling water pollution in densely settled areas were inadequate. Pressure for change came from at least two different sources. First, the increase in the incidence of disease caused many citizens to demand better water quality. Antipollution forces urged the adoption of statewide laws in the hope that a larger political unit might produce stricter enforcement. Second, disputes between municipalities concerning upstream polluters' responsibility for degrading the downstream environment provided additional impetus for invoking state authority. Consequently, beginning around the turn of the century, new water-pollution-control legislation was passed in many of the more populous states. For the most part, air-pollution control remained a local problem until much later.

Early attempts to improve the condition of the environment, whether local attempts to control smoke emitted by stationary sources or state efforts to reduce the human health hazards from raw sewage discharged into its waterways, were weakened by common problems. Vagueness in the wording of statutes and regulations was a primary weakness, as exemplified in the following two statutes:

> The emission of dense smoke from the smokestack of any boat or locomotive or from any chimney anywhere within the city shall be . . . a public nuisance.[4]
>
> No person shall discharge or permit to be discharged into any fresh water any sewage, excremental matter, domestic refuse or other pollution matter.[5]

Important questions are implicit in the wording of such public policies. First and foremost is the problem of definition. What is meant by "dense smoke" or "polluting matter"? Since the framers of the statute made no attempt to define these terms, enforcing authorities assumed the burden of convincing the courts that the administrator's perception of emissions was accurate and demonstrated a violation of the law. This vagueness in wording opened enforcement efforts to charges of arbitrary and capricious interpretation, which itself fostered policies of inaction. Cases brought to the courts under such amorphous legislation led to the same balance of interests that had earlier occurred in private damage suits. Judges often took the view that the public benefit obtained through the activity of an individual polluter, whether a municipal sewage-treatment plant or a steel-manufacturing plant, was more significant than any loss or damage to the community from pollution. The enforcement agent had to demonstrate first, that pollution was indeed being caused, and second, that the individual polluter brought before the court was responsible for it. Defendants could and often did make the two-pronged defense 1) that there was no problem, and 2) that the problem was caused by multiple sources of emissions and was not their responsibility alone. Little pollution abatement was accomplished with this type of regulation. In addition to problems brought on by lack of precise definitions, the greatest defect of such regulations was their case-by-case, after-the-fact approach to the problem. Few systematic efforts were made to analyze all sources of pollution and crack down on all offenders under these laws. In many cases, cries of inequity were justified.

## REGULATION BY PERMIT: THE PRESENT POLICY

The permit system, in theory at least, does provide for preventive action. Developed after the difficulties of the case-by-case approach became evident, it is today the single most important method used by states to control water-pollution problems and air pollutants from stationary sources. Many industrialized states with severe environmental problems enacted water-discharge permit laws early in the twentieth century. Others did not follow suit until much later, some not until legislative action on the federal level influenced them to do so. Starting in the 1950s, some states began applying the permit-system approach to stationary air-pollution sources as well, but because the federal government did not develop an air-pollution policy until well after its interest in water pollution was established, many statewide air-pollution statutes have later dates than their analogous water-pollution-control laws.

This early Maryland water-pollution-control law illustrates regulation by permit:

> After April 16, 1914, the State, a county, municipality, district, corporation, company, institution, or person shall not install a system of water supply, sewerage, or refuse disposal, for public use, nor materially alter or extend any such existing system without having received a written permit from the State Board of Health to do so; nor shall any permit for this purpose be issued until complete plans and specifications for the installation as the State Board of Health may require, have been submitted and approved by the Board.[6]

This type of regulation, although an improvement over earlier efforts toward pollution control, presented its own problems. Some state laws made it a punishable offense to discharge wastes without permits, but others merely stipulated that plans should be submitted for approval by the state board of health. Even if approval were not forthcoming, there was no legal penalty to stop the discharger from proceeding with the construction of his sewage system or factory. In many states, the new permit system merely created a ritual performed by municipal officials and industrial managers. Frequently this involved no more than mailing a permit application that was mechanically granted without official investigation of what was actually being deposited into the air or waterways of the state.

Under considerable pressure from the federal government, which had passed its first water-pollution-control law in 1948, the Association of State and Interstate Water Pollution Control Administrators attempted to standardize and strengthen state laws by drafting a model code.[7] After the passage of the first federal air-pollution law in 1955, the same type of process was repeated for state air-pollution laws. Gradually the states adopted many of the provisions of the model codes. By the 1970s all state laws contained at least some provisions of the models.

Such laws now grant authority to issue not only permits for new construction that may pollute the air or water but also operating permits for old and new facilities, which must be renewed periodically. This authority is delegated to either the Department of Health or Natural Resources, or to a recently created state environmental-protection agency modeled after the federal EPA. Additional powers are needed, however, if permits are to prove effective. Most pollution-control agencies now have the power to draft comprehensive water- and air-pollution-control plans for the state and to set actual environmental-quality standards. In practice this means that maximum concentrations for such pollutants as phosphates, expressed in parts per million (ppm) parts of water, are established for each body of water. The amounts of such substances as sulfur oxides that a given volume of air should contain are also restricted. These standards may be absolute limits at any point in time, but often they are expressed as average concentrations over a designated period of time, such as hours or even months.

Together the powers to formulate plans and set standards eliminate the need to prove that a state of pollution exists. Whenever the minimum amount of dissolved oxygen permissible in a river or the maximum hydrocarbon concentration permissible in air has been quantified for example, an antipollution agency has only to test air or water quality periodically in order to determine whether standards have been met. These powers do not settle the old arguments about multiple sources of pollution and inability to assess blame for any given problem, but if water or air quality is demonstrably substandard, state agencies with the power to create plans and standards no longer need to demonstrate that "pollution," defined as that which creates a hazard to public health, exists.

A separate enforcement section in most antipollution laws is directed at potential violators and expressly prohibits them from constructing or operating waste-discharging systems without a valid permit from the enforcement agency. It would seem that this prohibition is all that is necessary for a smoothly functioning pollution-control program—provided, of course, that the administering agency is sufficiently manned and funded. Armed with the knowledge of what does exist (actual air or water quality) and what should exist (standards), the administrators should be capable of calculating how much waste can be dumped into an area without degrading the environment below the standards set. By restricting each permit to allow only a specified strength and volume of discharge, the agency can limit the total waste load from all dischargers to that assimilable by the receiving water or air.

No pollution-control law, however, would be complete without its variance section. This portion of the law is broadly worded in most cases, as in this excerpt from the relatively strict Illinois Environmental Protection Act:

> The [Pollution Control] Board may grant individual variances beyond the limitations prescribed in this Act, whenever it is found, upon presentation of adequate proof, that compliance with any rule or regulation, requirement or order of the Board would impose an arbitrary or unreasonable hardship.
>
> . . . Such variance may be extended from year to year by affirmative action of the Board, but only if satisfactory progress has been shown.[8]

Such modifying clauses in all regulatory statutes provide the discretion needed to allow enforcement agencies to adjust their demands on violators in order to achieve individual justice and obtain voluntary compliance. They also provide ample opportunity for abuse of administrative discretion to produce favoritism and injustice. In effect, such clauses leave it to the total discretion of the enforcement agents to determine how closely any individual permit holder will be held to the provisions of his permit.

## IMPLEMENTATION: ADMINISTRATIVE REALITIES IN ENFORCEMENT

In practice the reality of enforcement has been quite different from the model. Rather than stipulating permissible levels of pollutant discharge, most permits in the past have been broadly worded, allowing the discharger to dump practically anything once the permit has been issued. Environmental-quality standards were set as a goal and permits were issued to dischargers, but few administrative-enforcement links were made between the two. In some states, however, more sophisticated permit systems contain specific restrictions; normally, these are expressed in terms of percentage reductions of wastes rather than in absolute amounts of permissible waste discharges. For example, the state may permit a municipal sewage-treatment plant to discharge whatever effluent it produces each day provided that it reduces the biochemical oxygen demand (BOD) by eighty percent instead of prohibiting it from discharging no more than fifty pounds of BOD per day. Standards based on such percentage reductions of emissions or effluents will produce the desired environmental quality if the administrative agency has sufficient information about total waste loads and assimilative capacity. But a state agency may also go through all the logical steps already outlined and find that some (or all) of its waste dischargers who have permits are not meeting the requirements.

In such cases, what recourse does the state agency have? The answer, as stated in the law, is the authority of the responsible agency to issue enforcement orders requiring that better results be obtained either through the installation of new pollution-abatement equipment or improvement of the old. Theoretically, most state agencies have the authority to require offenders to keep emissions within the limits of their permits or to require them to cease all discharges. In practice, such power is seldom used and few states issue many orders.[9] Instead, they make an effort to convince the operators that they ought to comply with the permits under which they now act. One additional sanction that the agencies can use to bolster their moral suasion is the refusal to renew any permits that are currently not being complied with, and even more realistically, the refusal to issue the new permits required for additional plant capacity unless the operating requirements for the wastes now being processed are met.

In most states the device of the enforcement order remains the ultimate sanction, regardless of how infrequently it is used. According to most state laws, the responsible agency may invoke this procedure whenever it has reason to believe that a violation of any provision of the law has occurred. Such an admonition leaves a considerable amount of discretion to the administering officials. The procedure may be triggered through the normal process of reviewing permits, studying operating reports, and conducting inspections. It may also follow periodic analyses of the air or bodies of water, or be instigated by individual complaints from private citizens.

Regardless of how initiated, several steps normally intervene between the first recognition of a problem and the court injunction forcing the polluter to cease and desist—steps that may consume many months or even several years and often are never completed. First, informal conciliation is usually tried by "informing" the polluter of the problem and asking for his voluntary cooperation. The discharger himself may ask for a hearing if he believes that the initial notification of a violation is wrong or unfair. Second (and more frequently), the administrative agency may call the violator before a public hearing if he has not taken the action requested within a certain amount of time. After the hearing, the agency issues an order. This order normally contains a time schedule with various enumerated steps, including deadlines for obtaining an engineering plan, for beginning construction, and a final date when the treatment facility should be in operation. The discharger at whom the order is aimed may still obtain modifications to the order if he can convince the enforcing agency that economic or technical contingencies necessitate modifications. He can obtain these changes without recourse to a public hearing, and numerous modifications to an order that was originally lauded in the press for its strictness may go into effect without mention in or knowledge of the media.

In practice, the polluter has the option of ignoring the order during the time period in which he ought to be making the alterations in his operation, and waiting for the attorney general of the state to take him to court. This may or may not ever happen, depending on the law of the state, the relationship between the administrative agency in charge of pollution control and the attorney general's office, and the latter's interest in pollution control. There is, of course, the hope that the court will ultimately find in favor of the violator, in which case his noncompliance has been vindicated. In any case, the polluter may consider the duration of the court case as another time period during which nothing need be done to comply with the order. Third and last, the polluter may decide that any fine imposed by the court is a modest sum in comparison with the cost of cleaning up, in which case there remains the ultimate sanction of a court injunction against the polluter to prevent his continuing the discharge. Once again, the administrative agency faces the problem of enforcing such an injunction through a contempt-of-court citation against any organization that simply refuses to cease and desist. Despite the hue and cry over pollution, examples are rare of a police authority stepping in to halt physically the flow of sewage from a municipal plant or emissions from industrial smokestacks.[10]

## LACK OF IMPACT FROM STATE PROGRAMS: TWO EXAMPLES

The crucial question is not what the regulations for controlling pollution provide but what kind of protection has resulted from these laws for the health and welfare of the people living in potentially hazardous environments. This question was vividly answered for residents of Chicago's south side in the spring of 1974. There, on April 26, a storage tank owned by Bulk Terminals Company and containing 500,000 gallons of silicon tetrachloride sprang a leak at about 12:30 P.M. At first company officials ordered employees to hose the tank down with water, an action which resulted in the release of toxic hydrochloric acid and silicic acid into the atmosphere. By the time the fire department was notified, the highly toxic fumes had blanketed the entire neighborhood and the fire and police departments could do nothing to plug the leak. Officials from city, state, and federal environmental-protection agencies came to view the growing clouds of acid vapor and discuss what could be done, without result. Downwind of Bulk Chemicals in the crowded Altgeld Gardens public-housing project, residents retched, choked, clawed at their streaming eyes, rolled on the ground in agony, and fled.[11]

More than twenty-four hours after the leak had begun, a U.S. Army Technical Escort Center group, summoned by EPA from the Aberdeen Proving Grounds in Maryland, arrived with rubber suits and other equipment needed to approach close enough to the disaster to pour cement into the hole. During the week that followed, firemen, city workers, and chemical experts from around the country dumped truck loads of crushed limestone and sand into the pool of chemicals around the tank to neutralize the acids, and spread 1,000 gallons of fuel oil over the surface of the pool to keep more vapors from rising into the air. Finally the remainder of the dangerous liquid was drained from the tank.[12]

Fortunately, no fatalities resulted directly from inhalation of the fumes, although hundreds of people were treated at hospitals and some were hospitalized for as much as a week after the incident. Thousands were evacuated from the area, and thanks to heroic efforts by the Chicago police and fire departments and especially to concern shown by neighbors, no one was left behind, no matter how young, old, ill, or disabled. At another time and another place, the residents might not be so lucky. Is this then the best response of which environmental-protection officials are capable: calling up the army and evacuating people?

Clearly the Illinois Environmental Protection Agency has greater statutory power than it used in this incident. Its enabling legislation provides:

> In other cases in which the Agency finds that an emergency condition exists creating an immediate danger to health, the Agency may seal any equipment, vehicle, vessel, aircraft, or other facility contributing to the emergency condition.[13]

Surely there is no argument that an emergency condition existed on the far south side of Chicago on April 26, 1974. Several agencies had the authority to step in and stop the leak if company officials were unwilling or unable to do so. What good does such authority do, however, when the administering agency lacks the equipment, training, or expertise to act? Emergency clauses, which are commonplace in pollution-control acts, are useless when the agency involved is impotent, for whatever reason.

City and state officials had proved themselves unable to protect the health and lives of black, south-side Chicago residents. A little earlier the same year, county and state officials manifested the same kind of indifference to the needs of more affluent suburban residents in outlying western areas. There an abandoned uncovered well, located on land owned by the Birdsong Buildings Co., Inc. was discovered to be the source of contaminated water that had been seeping into private wells and public water supplies in nearby Darien, Illinois. This time no army engineers were needed. Once the trouble was located state EPA and Dupage County health officials were able to plug the source by sealing the well. The numerous cases of diarrhea and vomiting which had given rise to the search for contaminated water could not, of course, be traced directly to the well, but it was hoped that the sealing of the well would eventually take care of the problem. Meanwhile, those householders who did not obtain water from public supplies, which were to be heavily chlorinated in the interim, were advised "to continue boiling their water for the next several months."[14]

In both these cases, public officials aided the citizens suffering the injury caused by pollution only after the fact. For many individuals this assistance came in the form of advice about self-help. In both incidents previously described, the effects suffered by citizens were the first indication of the presence of pollution for the responsible public officials. And the only "solution" offered to the victims was to avoid the problem either through evacuation of their homes or boiling their water.

In the chemical-storage-tank and uncovered-well emergencies, the private businesses from whose property the problems arose evidenced ignorance of their potential threat to the community and seemed cavalierly unconcerned about the danger. Many politicians urged an investigation and more restrictive legislation after the Chicago near-disaster; but after the publicity died down the responsible officials returned to their comfortable attitude of indifference. Environmental-protection officials seemed willing to let the wrongdoers go scot-free despite a clear injunction in the Illinois law prohibiting the creation of a health hazard to the population by contributing either to air or water pollution. The only sanction likely to result from the Chicago case awaits the outcome of court actions on the numerous private damage suits filed in the aftermath. If Bulk Terminals sees fit to take more precautions in storing dangerous chemicals on its property in the future, they are probably more concerned about civil suits than about any threat posed by a public enforcement agency.

It is not surprising that these two incidents occurred within a few months of each other, since the potential for similar accidents exists in every community of any size in the United States. The two cases could be dismissed on the premise that accidents do happen; the perpetrators of the danger to public health were in fact not violating any permit issued directly by an environmental-protection agency. Neither company was in the business of continuously emitting pollutants into the air or water, the major activity the Illinois EPA is designed to control. Companies do not have to apply for air-pollution permits to store dangerous chemicals, for it is assumed that they will not release dangerous substances into the air that citizens must breathe. Nevertheless, it is necessary for individuals to have permits to store dangerous chemicals in the city of Chicago, and such a permit was in force at the time of the Bulk Chemicals leak.

In those cases where continuous emissions are a problem the permit system should work more effectively, yet throughout August of that same year the media daily broadcast intermittent warnings and alerts about the level of ozone in the metropolitan area around Chicago. While enforcement agencies on the city, county, state, and federal levels quibbled about what constituted the danger threshold for ozone, the extremely young, old, pregnant, and infirm were warned against outdoor exercise. Although some industries publicly professed to having cut back operations in the public interest, no official sanction was taken against any contributor to the problem.[15] Official action was again restricted to putting the burden of finding a solution on those most likely to be hurt. The existing authority did not further restrict permits, withdraw variances, or even seal offending sources under conditions of emergency. The most vulnerable members of the city's population had to protect themselves as best they could. What would constitute a real emergency was left to conjecture, but obviously it would have to threaten more than sufferers from respiratory ills and others who apparently are considered marginal members of society by policy makers.

## POLITICAL AND ECONOMIC CONSTRAINTS ON ENFORCEMENT

The types of incidents recorded in the last section continue to occur with regularity around the nation, not just in the Chicago metropolitan area. Illinois is one state with serious pollution problems and some of the strictest laws dealing with pollution. The question remains: Why, with the statutes that now exist on the books, has the impact of pollution-control policy been no greater than it has? It is sometimes possible to buy permits, delays, and variances as needed, yet all the blame cannot fall on venal public officials interested only in lining their own purses at the public's expense.

There are two major types of polluters: private businesses and industries such as those involved in the Chicago area cases, and municipal authorities. The authorities often have a stake in adhering to air- and water-quality standards and most have their own local environmental-control agencies. Local governments are nevertheless often among the worst polluters when performing equally important official functions, the elimination of sewage and the generation of power when utilities are municipally owned. State administrators frequently consider them exempt from strong enforcement tactics simply because of the political ties between political leaders of communities and their state counterparts. A state politician who is dependent on the support of party leaders in large metropolitan areas is rarely eager to unleash his enforcement agents against his colleagues.

Even when state and local governments represent different parties or ideological factions within the same party, they are often sympathetic to one another's problems. State officials are aware that city officials face limited revenues and constantly rising costs for basic services. Sewage treatment does not rank high when it must compete with services such as education and police and fire protection. Despite the recent outcry over all forms of environmental degradation in our society there is still considerable resistance to bond issues for increasing the capacity or efficiency of city sewage-treatment plants. State officials are well aware that when city budgets become strained city officials consider the state legislature as the first source of relief. Why should they, therefore, add to the likelihood of such a request by further burdening city budgets?

Throughout the 1960s state pollution-control agencies in general tended to have more effect on public than on private polluters, even in the face of these problems. Municipalities received more permits and injunctions and offered more cooperation than did either private businesses or industries.[16] State officials knew much less about industrial pollution because of manufacturers' reluctance to divulge information about their processes. Until very recently many state officials were unaware of what the industrial giants were putting into the air and water in their jurisdictions. Politically, state indulgence of industrial and business polluters is easy to understand. Each state has an individual set of environmental-quality standards and its own enforcement agency. Polluters, therefore, have a useful weapon against any individual state government—the simple suggestion that they may find a more attractive location elsewhere if that state administration insists on stringently enforcing its regulations. Faced with the threat of losing industries to less forceful states, enforcement officials may choose a more conciliatory approach to polluters.

Although one might expect relatively underindustrialized states to find themselves less subject to such pressures, economic underdevelopment and a desire both to attract more industry and to retain what industry they have increases the pressure on these states. In order to make itself more attractive to industrial investors, a state's logical strategy is to develop a lax enforcement policy toward polluters. One blandishment often suggested to potential investors is the fact that natural resources are cheap, plentiful, and relatively unused, a suggestion that implies to most industrialists, experienced in reading cues, that they need pay little attention to pollution control. Until recently, industries leaving the older industrial areas of the northeast have been enticed by states in the southeast by the suggestion that not only labor but also land and water are available and inexpensive.

A natural ally for industrialists is found within the state governments themselves, commonly in the Departments of Natural Resources, which have traditionally thought of themselves as responsible for attracting new industry for the good of the state. Only recently has there been any hint that considerations other than increased productivity were relevant to the concept of progress. Whether or not the Department of Natural Resources plays the role of attracting new industry to a formerly impoverished area or of trying to hold onto a decreasing industrial base, the arguments to public-policy makers are likely to be the same: economic prosperity far outweighs other considerations. Periods of economic recession usually aggravate the situation, when competing administrative units perceive their fiscal problems most vividly.

Economic considerations do not always take precedence. The permit power has enabled some states and localities to make negative decisions concerning the siting of new industries in their areas in recent years. One example occurred in 1970 in a particularly poverty-stricken area on the coast of South Carolina. A German chemical company, Badische Anilin und Soda Fabrik, sought to locate a new plant there. Low-income commercial fishermen and luxury-resort owners combined forces with conservationists to delay the granting of a state-discharge permit until the company found a different site. Although many local officials felt the new plant would have eased the unemployment problems of Beaufort County's poor, those property owners concerned with pollution of Port Royal Sound proved the stronger influence in this instance.[17] Similar decisions were made in New Hampshire when local residents objected to Aristotle Onassis' proposal to locate a deep-water terminal for oil tankers off their unpolluted shores, and again in Denver when the population turned down an opportunity to host the 1974 Winter Olympics. In all three cases an economic bonanza for at least a portion of the population was rejected in favor of a less degraded environment, and although the issue was confounded by the fact that the expansionist forces were foreign and could thus be viewed as an outside threat to the local inhabitants, clearly some portion of the local population would have benefitted economically. To this day some groups no doubt regret these decisions.

## REDEFINING PRESENT POLICY: IMPLICATIONS FOR THE FUTURE

Present policy decisions do not pertain only to new potential polluters, who are now on notice that they will be expected to do more to reduce emissions than did their predecessors. Most areas with large populations and considerable current pollution have the greater problem of bringing traditional violators into line with the new laws. Issuing new permits for old behavior patterns is not the answer. One useful weapon of enforcement agencies is the public hearing, at which private citizens become informed about specific activities that pollute their environment. Adverse publicity may influence municipal officials and industrialists to increase their treatment efforts without the need to invoke sanctions. At other times municipal and business leaders may utilize all the delaying tactics outlined earlier. Some never consider any other response. Others may wish to comply with state laws, but are prevented from doing so out of fear of reactions from their constituents or stockholders.

Most state-enforcement actions rarely go beyond initial notification to the violator. Although economic and political considerations doubtless play a role in their decisions, most state agencies claim to be able to obtain cooperation at that stage. Many enforcement officials believe that if they cannot obtain voluntary compliance there is little purpose served in going on to the court stage.[18] In other words, it is simpler and more effective to persuade violators to take action than to attempt to coerce them. Over the years different patterns ranging from strict enforcement to nonenforcement have evolved among the fifty states. One variable affecting such patterns is the attitudes toward pollution control held by individual decision makers inside administrative agencies, whose discretionary authority influences the implementation of state policy.

In addition to personal attitudes, other factors also affect enforcement patterns. Even when a state agency head initiates an unusually activist enforcement policy, other authoritative decision makers may effectively stymie the program. State attorneys may refuse to prosecute many cases vigorously and judges may prove highly sympathetic to economic-hardship arguments of defendants. In such instances, it is inaccurate to say that there is a concerted state policy to force polluters to comply with the law. Whenever the outcome of court cases discourages prosecutors from bringing other similar cases to court, judges' decisions constitute a better indicator of public policy in that state than do administrative decisions.

The passage of a law does not terminate the role of state legislators in policy formulation. Individual legislators may still intervene on behalf of constituent polluters in order to have abatement orders changed and variances granted. In some states they may not need to do so on a continuing basis, because enforcement agents are inhibited by the potential for legislators' interference with administrative processes and have long ago adjusted their behavior accordingly. Many judges and state legislators may be more enthusiastic about enforcement of pollution-control laws than are the enforcers themselves, however, and in such cases, the watchdog function of the legislature and judiciary serves to strengthen administrative resolve.

If we were to conclude our analysis with a reading of the preamble to any state law, we would know very little about state environmental policy. These laws usually make a very general commitment to the principle of "restoring, protecting, and enhancing the quality of the environment."[19] In practice there is considerable room for slippage between the formal rule and the reality of implementation.

In some states, where administering agencies have liberally issued permits and variances to dischargers and ignored many of their own powers, there is no realistic public policy for controlling pollution. The policy of the state must then be defined as whatever the enforcement agency has chosen to make of it. In those states where administrators hold to the belief that it is useless to take violators to court, public policy on pollution control is the outcome of negotiations undertaken periodically by waste dischargers and administrators. In states that frequently hold public hearings, all participants who appear regularly before hearing examiners, including the mass media, are included in the bargaining process and may help to shape policy.

Even if the net effect of such political influences on the public-policy process is measurable, further questions concerning the impact of policy arise: What is the actual effect of law-enforcement efforts on the quality of air and water in the states? If the quality has steadily deteriorated since the passage of the law in question, does it matter that the state has a public policy designed to "improve or maintain" its environment? The logical argument is that were it not for the policy of control, environmental quality would have become even more degraded in the same period of time. Many waste dischargers also argue publicly that they are clean living folk who would have done their best for clean air and water without the heavy hand of government intervention. If their treatment facilities would have produced the same quality of discharge regardless of the terms of their permits or the conscientiousness of state officials, then indeed public policy in this area is irrelevant. The present state of the environment is instead entirely due to the cumulative effect of many private decisions made by waste dischargers; but given dischargers' reactions to most laws and regulations created by public bodies, these private decision makers would be unlikely to voluntarily make much effort to clean up their own wastes. Because no data exists for such hypothetical situations, questions about what the condition of the environment would be like without controls will remain unanswered.

More important than arguments about what might have been are present differences of opinion about what *does* exist. Experts differ on whether the air and water have improved or become more degraded in the last five years. The range of environmental quality around the United States makes it entirely possible that both sides are right, depending on the location of the sampling. Many polluters now argue that whatever benefits have been obtained from pollution controls have not been worth the cost to society, and call for a reassessment of present laws and standards.[20] Environmentalists argue that the fight has only begun. They feel that little has been done to clean up the condition of the environment on the state level, and, dissatisfied with the status quo, they have turned to the national government.

## SUMMARY

Land-pollution control is presently in a transitional state, moving from local to state control in many areas—a phase in development through which water- and air-pollution policy passed several years ago. Generally, events in the development of air- and water-pollution policy have paralleled each other in recent years and are predictive of what is likely to occur in the land-use area in the future. What began as an ad hoc regulatory process has been gradually strengthened, until today most state laws depend on a permit system under which all dischargers must register with the state pollution-control agency and obtain permission to dump wastes into the state's natural resources.

Some states have pioneered in the permit-system program and served as models for others; many have waited until forced by federal legislation to take action. Despite obvious differences, no single state program is without problems and none has succeeded in producing the kind of environment that antipollution interests would like to see. Polluting interests have effectively utilized procedural safeguards designed to protect potential law violators to delay, and in some cases to weaken, the net effect of these laws. Like most administrative laws directed at nonviolent crimes, antipollution laws have been administered in a more conciliatory fashion than those directed toward crime in the streets. This divergence in administration is due largely to the economic and political influence that violators wield with law-enforcement agents, courts, and state legislators. Whatever the cause, the fact remains that the dissatisfaction of antipollution interests has resulted in an increasing demand for action at the national rather than the state level.

## NOTES

1. Kenneth E. F. Watt, "Planning—So There Will Be a Future," in *Ecocide . . . and Thoughts Toward Survival*, ed. Clifton Fadiman and Jean White (Palo Alto, Calif.: James E. Freel, 1971), pp. 109–39.

2. Luther J. Carter, "Land Use: Rules Panel and Nixon Leave House Bill in Limbo," *Science* 183 (March 22, 1974): 1176–78.

3. *New York Times*, July 9, 1974, p. 17.

4. Egbert Jamison and Francis Adams, eds., *Municipal Code of Chicago for 1881* (Chicago: Beach, Bernard & Co., 1881), p. 386. This also provided for a fine of between $5 and $50 for ordinance violations. Naturally this regulation has been amended numerous times since 1881.

5. New Jersey, *Annotated Statutes* (1966), Title 58:10:5. The New Jersey statutes have been amended several times since this law was created in 1901, but the original wording at the beginning of the act has been retained.

6. Maryland, *Annotated Code* (1957), Article 43:385.

7. For the terms of this model code, see U.S. Department of the Interior, Federal Water Pollution Control Administration, *Suggested Water Pollution Control Act*, revised, 1965.

8. Illinois Environmental Protection Act, House Bill 3799, 1970 Legislature, as amended by House Bills 785 and 1844, 1971 Legislature; amended July 1, 1972, Section 35.

9. In December 1959 the House Committee on Public Works of the U.S. Congress administered a questionnaire about the use of administrative orders to control water pollution. The results of this questionnaire were published in U.S. Congress, House of Representatives, "A Study of Pollution—Water," *A Staff Report to the Committee on Public Works*, 88th Congress, 1st session, 1963, p. 98. A total of 4,795 orders were issued in FY 1959. The author compiled the number of orders issued in FY 1969 by personally questioning individual state water-pollution-control agencies, and the comparable figure was 1,803 orders issued that year. Given the fact that there were over 50,000 discharging plants against which orders might have been issued in that year, this results in an average of less than .03 order per plant in FY 1969.

10. In December 1971 the federal EPA obtained a court order directing certain industries in Birmingham, Alabama to cease operations due to severely polluted conditions after state authorities had failed to act.

11. *Chicago Tribune*, April 27–May 5, 1974.

12. Ibid.

13. Illinois Environmental Protection Act, House Bill 3788, 1970 Legislature, as amended by House Bills 785 and 1844, 1971 Legislature; amended July 1, 1972, Section 35(b).

14. *Chicago Tribune*, February 1, 1974, area 1, p. 1.

15. *Chicago Tribune*, August 8, 1974, p. 2.

16. The author conducted research into both these and other aspects of the enforcement process and found that states almost uniformly enforce the laws more strictly for public organizations than for private groups. See Lettie McSpadden Wenner, "Enforcement of Water Pollution Laws in the U.S.," unpublished Ph.D. dissertation, University of Wisconsin, 1971. See also Lettie McSpadden Wenner, "Enforcement of Water Pollution Control Laws in the U.S.," *Law and Society Review* (May 1973).

17. *New York Times*, February 1, 1970, p. 7; February 12, 1970, p. 50.

18. In May 1972 the author conducted a mailed survey of 221 state water-control officials. A control group of federal administrators was also polled. When presented

with the statement: "Water-pollution-control law-enforcement agencies will obtain better results by persuading dischargers to comply than by law suits," seventy-six percent of the state people agreed with it, whereas only forty-one percent of the federal officials did. See Lettie McSpadden Wenner, "Attitudes of Water Pollution Control Officials," monographed, Center for Governmental Studies, Northern Illinois University, January 1973.

19. See, for example, Illinois Environmental Protection Act, House Bill 3788, 1970 Legislature, as amended by House Bills 785 and 1844, 1971 Legislature; amended July 1, 1972, Section 2 (b).

20. The ink on the Oregon statute against nonreturnable beverage containers was scarcely dry before attempts to rescind it were initiated. Other examples include the 1971 Delaware Coastal Zone Act, which prohibits heavy industry and offshore unloading facilities in that state. It was under severe attack all through 1974 by business and the building trades. *New York Times*, March 10, 1974, p. 3.

CHAPTER FIVE

# Pollution Control: Evolving Federal Policy

Like air, water, and land pollution, environmental policies at the local, state, and federal levels are inextricably intertwined. Initiatives taken at the national level have been influential in shaping policy at lower levels of government (see chapter four); thus an output (policy) from one level of government has considerable impact and is a significant input to the policy-making process at other levels. The decisions of different states have been instrumental in initiating new federal legislation. Some state laws, such as the California statute controlling both stationary and vehicular sources of air pollution, have served as models for federal legislation. More often, environmentalists have been dissatisfied with state policy outputs and have subsequently shifted their demands to the federal level. The history of pollution control in the United States, like many other public-policy issues, has been a story of increasing federal assumption of authority. For those satisfied with state policy outputs this has been a needless assumption of power. For those dissatisfied with state and local policy outputs, it has symbolized the only means left to achieve their goals.

## RIVERS AND HARBORS ACT OF 1899

Just as most people would be surprised to learn how long ago the first municipal and state antipollution laws were passed, most would also be shocked to learn that there exists a nineteenth-century federal "water-pollution-control law." In point of fact the "antipollution" aspect of the Refuse Act (also called the Rivers and Harbors Act of 1899) was primarily for the purpose of keeping the carcasses of cows and other floating debris from obstructing the flow of commerce in navigable waters at a time when water transport was more important to our nation's economy than it is today. The act did, however, contain one section that could be and was interpreted broadly in the early 1970s as an antipollution clause by some imaginative conservation lawyers and politicians and by some courts:

> It shall not be lawful to throw, discharge, or deposit . . . any refuse matter of any kind or description whatever other than that flowing from streets and sewers and passing therefrom in a liquid state into any navigable water of the United States. . . .
>
> Provided that the Secretary of the Army . . . may permit the deposit of any material above mentioned in navigable waters, within limits to be defined and under conditions to be prescribed by him.[1]

This law is remarkably similar to many present state laws that establish the right of the state authorities to issue permits for dumping into waterways today, with one important difference: The 1899 law explicitly exempts from control all sewage from municipal sewer lines. But the law has been interpreted to include all industrial, commercial, and other nonpublic liquid wastes, even when they reach the waterways through conduits constructed for that purpose. Because state water-pollution-control programs in the 1960s were least effective in controlling private effluents, environmentalists came to pin their hopes on this old federal law for controlling industrial pollutants.

Despite the existence of the 1899 law, no comprehensive permit system had ever regulated the discharge of industrial effluents into navigable waterways of the United States. What the drafting committee had in mind when it passed the 1899 statute remains forever dimmed by the passage of time. The responsible enforcement agency (the U.S. Army Corps of Engineers) interpreted it to be an attempt at facilitating navigation rather than improving the quality of water. During the first eighty years of the law's existence, the Corps of Engineers primarily used its authority to issue permits for two purposes: 1) to construct wharves, jetties, and other structures that protrude into navigable waters to aid navigation, and 2) to dump material dredged from navigable channels in order to prevent the obstruction of commerce.

For a few brief moments in the early 1970s it appeared that this historic piece of federal legislation marked the beginning of the first comprehensive federal effort to catalogue industrial sources of pollutants and bring them all under permit. Under pressure from numerous private lawsuits directed toward changing the federal government's implementation of the Act, the president issued an executive order instructing the secretary of the Army to initiate such a program.[2]

The much-delayed initiation of a federal permit program was cut short in the planning state, however, after approximately half of all industrial concerns discharging liquid wastes into the waterways of the United States had provided information about their discharges. Lawsuits filed by environmentalists precipitated this untimely end of a federal policy. Prompted by the fear that the federal government might issue blanket permits to all industries without any real restrictions, thereby preempting even weak state efforts to bring such dischargers under regulation, they argued that an environmental-impact statement for each federal permit must be filed under the new National Environmental Policy Act.[3] When the federal courts sustained their reasoning the executive branch dropped its efforts to begin issuing permits. Later, Congress passed the 1972 amendments to the Federal Water Pollution Control Act and formally eliminated the possibility of creating such a federal permit system under the old law.[4] Thus the argument over what policy should be with regard to enforcement of the 1899 Rivers and Harbors Act was resolved through the interaction of all three branches of government.

## COMPREHENSIVE FEDERAL LEGISLATION

The recent turmoil over the 1899 law left one question unanswered and for the most part unasked: Why did so many people involved with water-pollution control seek to utilize this early law when other more specific federal legislation for water-pollution control had existed since 1948? One explanation is the vagueness of the 1899 law, whose implications for environmental control went undetected by opponents of pollution control at the time of its passage. By the 1930s, however, the issue of water-pollution control was well on the way to becoming politicized. Conservationists were making their demands heard in the halls of Congress, while groups concerned with using water primarily for waste discharges were sufficiently alerted to protect their interests.

The debate lasted until 1948 (including a lengthy recess for the war), by which time Congress enacted a weak compromise bill.[5] Later accretions to the original act have been extensive and detailed; they too have been the result of rancorous arguments among different interests, all following a distinct pattern. Environmental groups, ranging from the League of Women Voters to the Audubon Society, appear before congressional subcommittees preceding

TABLE II
Comprehensive Federal Legislation

| Legislation | Date | Agency | Major Function | Enforcement Technique |
|---|---|---|---|---|
| Federal Water Pollution Control Act FWPCA | 1948 | PHS/HEW | Research and development | Notification to polluters |
| | 1955 | HEW | | Conference |
| | 1956 | | Grants-in-aid for: State enforcement; sewage treatment plant construction | |
| | 1965 | | | Authorization for states to set ambient-water quality standards |
| | 1966 | Department of the Interior | | Federal government authorized to initiate court cases after 180-day notice to dischargers |
| | 1967 | | | Water-quality standards deadline |
| | 1970 | EPA | | |
| | 1972 | | | Treatment technique mandated (to be defined by EPA) |
| | 1977 | | | Deadline for "best practicable"; secondary treatment for municipalities |
| | 1983 | | | Deadline for "best available"; "best practicable" for municipalities |
| | 1985 | | | No polluting-discharge goal |

| | | | | |
|---|---|---|---|---|
| Clean Air Act | 1955 | HEW | Research and development | Notification to polluters |
| | 1963 | | Grants-in-aid for state enforcement | Conferences |
| | 1965 | | Auto-emissions standards set by U.S. Congress | Certification of prototypes |
| | 1967 | | | Ambient-air-quality standards to be set by states in federally defined regions |
| | 1968 | | | First deadline for car-emissions standards |
| | 1970 | EPA | New auto-emissions standards set by Congress | National ambient-air-quality standards authorized by Congress; emission standards for new stationary sources authorized by Congress |
| | 1971 | | | EPA sets ambient-air standards for six pollutants |
| | 1972 | | | State implementation plans due |
| | 1973 | | | EPA sets emissions standards for four industries |
| | 1975 | | | First deadline for primary air-quality standards in some states (postponed) |
| | 1976 | | | Deadline for some car-emissions standards (postponed) |
| | 1982 | | | New deadline for air-quality standards |

passage of such amendments to argue in favor of the federal government's assumption of control over the program. Opposition to the bills is heavily weighted by industrial interests such as the National Association of Manufacturers and trade associations, but these are joined by many state and local officials arguing that they are capable of controlling their own pollution problems. Generally, the result of this debate has been to slowly increase federal authority.

Following closely on the heels of federal water-pollution legislation, air-pollution-control bills have assumed a similar pattern. Environmental and industrial forces have faced each other during debate over passage, and each new amendment has provided greater authority for the federal level, although this has proved a less tortuous process the second time around. The first federal air-pollution legislation was not passed until 1955 but it has been amended only four times.[6] In some cases Congress has been willing to extend federal authority in this area more quickly than it did with water pollution. The fact that air-pollution legislation has been able to build on the groundwork laid by the Federal Water Pollution Control Act gives to the history of air-pollution legislation a much abbreviated appearance, but its story essentially parallels that of water-pollution control a few years earlier (see Table II).

It was established early that individual states have first-refusal rights over both water- and air-pollution controls. Official recognition of this policy was manifested in both the Federal Water Pollution Control Act of 1948[7] and the Air Pollution Control Act of 1955.[6] Despite changes to both laws over the years, a similar policy statement has been retained at the beginning of each act:

> . . . it is hereby declared to be the policy of Congress to recognize, preserve, and protect the primary responsibilities and rights of the States in preventing and controlling water pollution.[8]

and

> . . . the prevention and control of air pollution at its source is the primary responsibility of States and local governments.[9]

This affirmation of public policy, the states' natural reluctance to give up prerogatives to the national government, and the relative balance between propollution and antipollution forces have combined to produce a federal policy that has only gradually increased in strength over a twenty-year period.

The frequent shifts in responsibility for federal-water pollution control during the first two decades of its history exemplify this gradual increase. The surgeon general and the Public Health Service originally administered the 1948 law. The increasing importance of this function was later recognized in two stages: First, the secretary of Health, Education, and Welfare assumed official responsibility for water-pollution control, and second, a new segment of HEW was created, the Federal Water Pollution Control Administration (FWPCA). In 1966 the administrative function was moved out of HEW entirely and lodged in the Department of the Interior until 1970 when a new independent agency without Cabinet status, the Environmental Protection Agency (EPA) was created. There, water-pollution-control experts joined air-pollution-control personnel, who had remained in the National Air Pollution Control Administration (NAPCA), a part of HEW, since the initiation of legislation in 1955. In EPA, also in 1970, an Office of Solid Wastes Management was created to deal with the third portion of residuals management heretofore untouched by federal law. Altogether, water-pollution control has fallen within four distinct administrative frameworks in its relatively brief history. These changes have come about primarily because of recognition of the increasing importance of environmental problems, but one unavoidable result has been a lack of program continuity. Present attempts to evaluate the success of environmental-control programs must be prefaced with the disclaimer that more lead time is needed before an impact can be measured.

## GRANTS-IN-AID: THE OPENING WEDGE

Initially faced with states' sensitivity to what they viewed as yet another federal intrusion into their domain, the federal programs began modestly enough by emphasizing a program with which few states' rights advocates could quarrel. The most important part of both the 1948 water and 1955 air laws, and one that gave impetus to the program, was the authority to provide research and technical assistance to states on specific pollution problems. Originally federal agencies were restricted to conducting research upon the request of state and local governments. Only later was this authority broadened to include federally initiated investigations into pollution problems involving more than one state. Enabling the federal government to contract out part of its research responsibilities to private industrial and university organizations, as well as to state and local government organizations, considerably sweetened the pot for opponents of the legislation. In addition, funds for outright grants for these purposes were provided. Today a portion of the Environmental Protection Agency's budget is still used for research and development of new technologies for handling air and water-pollution problems, but the major part of its program has been channeled in other directions.

The National Resource Recovery Act of 1970 places solid-waste management at approximately the same stage of development in the 1970s that water and air-pollution control occupied in the 1950s and early 1960s respectively. Federal funds are now available for experimental and demonstration projects for solid-waste recovery. In St. Louis, for example, a plant built by EPA grants uses up to thirty percent of the city's daily trash load to generate enough heat to replace ten percent of the coal normally burned by a local power plant.[10] Such recycling efforts are in the experimental stages, and for the most part they are neither economically profitable nor self-sustaining. The federal government, under the auspices of EPA, has undertaken other projects, such as encouraging the use of recycled materials by the federal government itself. But for the 1970s it is clear that solutions to solid-waste problems remain in the research and development stages.

A second type of federal grant available under present legislation, besides that for research, was not mentioned in either of the first two laws. Added in 1956 to the water law and in 1963 to the clean-air act, it now provides some federal funds to state agencies for meeting the costs of their own pollution-abatement programs. Ostensibly the laws require that federal administrators approve state plans for pollution control in order for the state to qualify for its share of the administrative expenses allocated by the federal government. This provision, however, in no way guarantees that all states will handle the problem in an equally effective manner. Despite this attempt to upgrade the states' efforts in the field of pollution control, allocators of federal funds have never seen fit to strip any given state of its allotment. To do so would reduce whatever influence federal officials have in the least effective of the state-enforcement agencies.

Compared with the modest funds available over the years for research and state-enforcement programs, a much more significant federal grant-in-aid program has been available since 1956 for the water-quality program; no comparable program exists for either air or solid wastes. Recognizing that one barrier to utilizing present technology for municipal sewage-treatment plants has been the paucity of funds at that governmental level, Congress began in 1956 to authorize the use of federal funds for such projects. Unlike the research and development budget, this program is designed not to seek new methods of handling sewage, but to apply on a large scale technology presently available. The history of this sewage treatment program graphically demonstrates the incremental nature of most government programs. At first the law limited the federal funds in any city's sewage-treatment project to a maximum of thirty percent, but this percentage has gradually been increased until the 1972 amendments to the law placed the federal share at seventy-five percent of the total amount. Congressional funding has increased over the years as well. Begun modestly enough at a level of $50 million a year in 1956, the amount of authorization for waste-water treatment plants has increased with each amendment to the original water-pollution-control act, rising to a level of $7 billion for fiscal year 1975.

What Congress authorizes for different programs and what is actually appropriated each year are frequently very different amounts. After the $150 million level was reached in 1966 a considerable discrepancy developed between authorization and appropriation. An extreme example of this phenomenon came in fiscal year 1970 when $1 billion were authorized by Congress, the Johnson administration subsequently asking for only $215 million.[11] Congress compromised and appropriated $800 million, which went unused while the Nixon administration debated the desirability of releasing these funds.

Starting in fiscal year 1972 President Nixon began the practice of impounding a portion of the reduced amount actually appropriated by Congress, so that by fiscal year 1974 the state agencies had received only half of the $7 billion originally authorized for distribution to municipalities applying for federal aid.[12] A considerable controversy arose over the legality of the president's use of impoundment, and eventually the U.S. Supreme Court agreed with municipal and state governments that all the funds should be released. This example illustrates once more the need to proceed with caution when defining public policy. Taken at face value, the Water Pollution Control Act amendments of 1972 define federal policy as the funding of sewage treatment plants at an annual level of $1 billion. Numerous factors have prevented that policy from becoming reality, and it is important to separate symbolic policy outputs from actual implementation.

Improvement of the quality of waterways throughout the United States was the declared policy goal for federally funded sewage treatment, as it was for other aspects of the Water Pollution Control Act. Applications for individual grants had to be justified by the degree to which they would contribute to the total clean-up effort. Implementation of the project has fallen short of its stated objectives, in part due to the way funds were distributed on both the federal and state levels.[13] On the federal level, the goal of cleaner water early conflicted with two other congressional goals: the political necessity of distributing federal largesse evenly among the states and the congressional desire to use public-works projects as a tool to relieve economically depressed areas. From the outset distribution of funds was therefore based partially on state population and economic need rather than on actual water conditions. On the state level, administrators often selected municipalities for grants on a "first come, first served" basis instead of rating the programs of different communities for effectiveness and incurring the wrath of local politicians.

Both allocation methods are politically understandable. They are, however, less than efficient in achieving the goal of clean water unless municipalities with less pressing economic problems are willing to take care of their own pollutants voluntarily. Given the natural inclination of local officials to take advantage of a federal-grant program if one exists, municipal responsibility is an unrealistic assumption, and some of the largest pollution problems have been ignored while the municipalities in question wait their turn for a grant. The "first come, first served" method may have a long-term cumulative effect on water quality if this method eventually meets all needs. In the meantime, there may be little discernible effect on waterways. If needs grow at a faster rate than federal funds become available or if states allow new industrial growth to "compensate for" cleaner municipal effluents, there may be no long-term positive effects either.

## FEDERAL ENFORCEMENT: CONFERENCE

Distribution of federal resources always creates controversy over the level of resource allocation and the manner of its distribution—how much money and who gets it? Such problems created by federal grant-in-aid programs, however, are minor compared with resistance generated by federal regulation of actual pollution-abatement programs. Those who want funds usually accept them without argument and restrict their complaints mainly to the nonavailability and low level of financing, rather than challenging the principle of undertaking the program at all. States have proved most jealous of their authority when confronted with federal enforcement of pollution abatement. Changes in federal-enforcement regulations have necessarily been even slower and more incremental than changes in funding grants (see Table II).

In 1948 and 1955 federal enforcement action was foreshadowed but dimly, and then only in interstate situations and with the consent of the states in which waste discharges were originating. Under the early laws federal administrators were empowered to "notify" persons they had reason to suspect of polluting and to bring this notification to the attention of the proper authorities within the states. If the notification had no effect on the polluters, the next notification to the state pollution-control agency might be "accompanied by a recommendation that it initiate a suit to abate the pollution in a court of proper jurisdiction."[14] If after another "reasonable time" (never defined) the state took no action against the alleged polluter, the federal government could hold a public hearing, out of which might come recommendations to the appropriate authorities who had hitherto failed to act under their own laws.

In 1956 a new enforcement technique was developed for water-pollution control and later extended to air pollution in 1963. Under the new federal authority HEW was empowered to call conferences on pollution either on its own initiative (whenever the health and welfare of the people in different states were involved) or at the request of the governor or pollution-control agency of any state—not necessarily the state from which the pollution was originating. State agencies responsible for pollution in their areas would receive the recommendations from the conference; after six months of failure to act the Secretary of HEW was then empowered to call a public hearing whose members could make recommendations for pollution abatement. If he chose to do so, the secretary could send such findings to the alleged polluters and to state and interstate pollution-control agencies. A reasonable time for action was specified, not less than six months. After the second six-month period had elapsed, HEW could request the Justice Department to file suit in federal court against individual polluters.

The utmost sanction was a charge of contempt of court that could be brought against a polluter only after a court had rendered judgment, issued an injunction, and then determined that its order had not been obeyed. The courts, however, were cautioned to give due consideration to the practicability and to the physical and economic feasibility of securing abatement of any pollution. Compared with the notification method of the earliest laws the conference technique increased the federal government's enforcement activity. From 1957 through mid-1972 there were sixty different water-pollution conferences. During the shorter period (from 1963 to 1970) when the conference was the major means of enforcement for air pollution, ten such enforcement conferences were held.[15] Most of these meetings were initiated by federal officials; the remainder, which were requested by governors, came only after subtle prodding by the federal agency.

The official participants in such conferences were limited to the state pollution-control agencies involved, plus any interstate agency with jurisdiction in the area, and the regional officials of HEW (later EPA) who had conducted an investigation of water or air quality prior to the conference. An official from Washington was usually sent out to chair the meeting and to act as moderator between opposing points of view. Early in the process, however, it became customary to allow other interested parties, polluters and antipollution forces alike, to make statements of their views to the conference in public session. At the end of each conference a summary statement, signed by all official conferees, was issued. By this means the conferees adopted recommendations that set out in detail the types of treatment needed to remedy the situation under investigation, the effluent or emission quality to be obtained from the treatment, and deadlines for the new or modified treatment facilities to be in operation. This summary statement, in effect, constituted an agreement by state pollution-control agencies that they would oversee the implementation of the various recommendations of the conference.[16]

All federal responsibility did not officially end when the states received the initiative to act. If the states did not take action by the end of a specified time period, the federal government might call a public hearing. HEW (later EPA) also had authority to request the attorney general to bring suit against individual polluters. The federal government obviously preferred not to invoke such authority, since the vast majority of pollution problems never got beyond the conference stage. A few reached public hearings, but only twice—once in the case of water and once for air—did federal officials feel sufficiently outraged to go to court. In 1961 a court order was obtained against the city of St. Joseph, Missouri, for polluting the Mississippi River, and in 1969 a suit was filed against a chicken-rendering plant in Bishop, Maryland, for polluting the air above Delaware.[17] The normal pattern was for a conference to meet and draw up recommendations to which the conferees agreed unanimously. Instead of holding a public hearing later the conference was often reconvened to determine whether the recommendations had been carried out by the responsible authorities.

Federal officials tended to rely on the rather weak weapon of public opinion at this stage in their attempt to add an enforcement "stick" to their grant-in-aid "carrot." Federal/state conferences were conducted with a maximum of publicity and usually drew much attention to the relative strictness or laxity of state pollution-control-law enforcement. By arousing the local media, federal conferences encouraged local antipollution forces to be more forceful in making their demands known to local and state officials. State officials would increase their own actions against polluters to the degree that they wanted to avoid further federal involvement in their state. Conferences also served as an additional source of authority for state officials. Intrastate conferences on particular problem areas often resulted in more effective abatement activity because of the threat of a federal investigation. One function of the federal-conference recommendation was to absorb a share of the pressure put on state enforcement agencies by municipal and industrial dischargers. Moving the decision-making process one level further from the interests being regulated reduced the influence of polluters.

During the 1960s federal officials rarely used the courts. Like their counterparts at the state level, federal officials preferred conciliation to hard-nosed law enforcement. Murray Stein, the chief federal-hearing examiner, stated at the 1967 Puget Sound hearings, "We strongly support the conference technique and we measure our success by the problems which are solved at the conference tables rather than in court."[18] This attitude was further spelled out by the same official at a later date:

> For any government to take legal action against one of its political subdivisions has always been a delicate problem under our system of jurisprudence. Obviously, a negotiated settlement based on mutual consent is infinitely preferable to legal proceedings.
>
> Experience with our specific water pollution problems has shown that an equitable solution can almost always be achieved if all parties approach the problem with goodwill, reasonableness, and respect for our democratic governmental process.[19]

What often happened was that the regulators and regulated met and discussed their mutual problems. State pollution-control officials occupied the dual role of apologist for their own municipal and industrial polluters and chief complainant against other states' pollution of shared resources. A third party, opponents of pollution—whether public-interest groups like the Environmental Defense Fund, economic interests such as resort owners, or ad hoc citizens' groups taking a transitory interest in the subject—played a formal role. They were given an opportunity to address the meeting and often did so at great length and with great emotion, appealing to participants to consider such esoteric values as natural beauty and the welfare of wildlife. Officials in charge of weighing private values to achieve the public good listened to such rhetoric with alternately bemused and embarrassed expressions.[20] They then returned to their primary task of conferring with polluters over technical problems and economic considerations in order to reach their conclusions.

The fact that the same individuals might from time to time represent different (and supposedly opposing) organizations added to this cooperative spirit. The same engineer who one year appeared as a technician for EPA might shortly become a state pollution-control agent whose role it was to explain why the federal recommendations for his state could not be carried out, or even a municipal or industrial engineer explaining the technical and economic difficulties of complying with any orders. The antipolluters, on the other hand, seemed to communicate primarily with themselves and the media. They received considerable television footage, but the effectiveness of their statements depended mostly on the repercussions such exposure had on the public at large and incumbent and office-seeking politicians in particular. Despite official care taken to provide for full representation of all interests in enforcement conferences, the major participants continued to be technicians who wore first one hat and then another. Antipollution forces remained tolerated, rather than influential, participants, and the concept of a balanced forum wherein all interests met to negotiate seemed somewhat contrived.

## AMBIENT-AIR- AND WATER-QUALITY STANDARDS

Until 1965 federal pollution control suffered from the same problem of vagueness under which state laws had so long languished. Pollution definition was uncertain, and beyond recognizing the fact that it had to do with endangering the health and welfare of the people, the relevant laws left unmentioned the criteria determining whether such danger existed. In each conference considerable time and energy were spent in arguing over whether the water or air under consideration was indeed polluted.

The 1965 amendments to the water-quality law made a first effort to establish objective criteria for judging the level of pollution in a body of water. Each state was given the responsibility for establishing water-quality standards for all interstate waterways in its jurisdiction. In the case of air pollution, this development did not occur until 1967 when the secretary of HEW was empowered to designate air-quality-control regions (primarily over and around metropolitan areas) that needed standards. States were now also given authority to establish actual air-quality standards, but if they did not choose to set ambient-air- and water-quality standards in the prescribed areas by the end of the stipulated time limit, the federal government was given power to do so. The secretary of HEW was to review and approve state standards, and he was empowered to call a standards-setting conference if the states did not comply. If a state's standards failed to obtain federal approval, HEW (later EPA) could promulgate alternatives.

Since one logical strategy in developing environmental standards is to look first to the prevalent conditions in any area, state standards often came to reflect a statement of what was rather than what should be. Standards varied radically in severity, and considerable argument arose over how strict was strict enough. To meet the problem of achieving comparable standards, the federal government initially took the stance that the present downward trend in environmental quality should not be continued. States were discouraged from setting standards lower than their current air and water quality—from aiming at a poorer environment than they already had. Such a policy clearly discriminated against the economic development of those states and locales that were relatively unindustrialized and underpopulated, for it could freeze them into a higher level of environmental quality than the goals of already polluted states. The less developed states did not often follow the federal government's advice. Eventually federal administrators established highly flexible guidelines that permitted standards to be lowered below present quality if justified by "necessary economic and social development."

Throughout negotiations over the level at which ambient-air and water quality should be set, it was clear that federal authorities were reluctant to utilize all the powers they had been given. Despite the 1967 deadline originally set for states' submission of water-quality standards, by April 1972 EPA was still listing some eight states as having only partially approved standards.[21] During the entire five years only one standards-setting conference was ever called—in April 1969 for certain sections of the Mississippi River.[22] Some legislators (urged on by environmentalists) who were well aware of the difficulties of formulating administrative policy in this manner were determined to make some changes.

Legislated changes came in 1970, and for the first time in the history of federal pollution control the innovation occurred first in the field of air quality rather than water quality. Until 1970 developments in air-pollution laws had followed and rather closely paralleled those in the Water Pollution Control act. In 1970, however, amendments to the Clean Air Act provided for nationally determined ambient-air standards. The administrator of EPA was given the authority to adopt primary and secondary air-quality standards for each air pollutant that in his judgment had an adverse effect on public health or welfare and for which EPA had previously issued advisory air-quality criteria to the states. Primary air standards should maintain the quality needed to protect the public health, while secondary standards should protect the public welfare (defined further as agriculture, property, and esthetic values). Secondary standards were stricter than primary ones, but primary standards would go into effect first. By April 1971 EPA had established primary and secondary national ambient-air-quality standards for six air pollutants: particulate matter, sulfur oxides, carbon monoxide, hydrocarbons, nitrogen oxides, and photochemical oxidants.[23]

Whether such ambient-air standards are good or bad, strict or lax, undoubtedly depends on one's perspective. As is certain to be the case in any national decision-making process, the outputs generated proved to be stricter than those some state agencies would have produced and less strict than the outputs of others. They are not so lax, however, as to be simply a statement of the lowest common denominator for American air quality, since the air quality in most metropolitan areas exceeds even the primary standards for some of the six pollutants covered.

Air-quality standards are not immutable and provision was made in the law for altering them in the future. By 1973 the process of revision had already begun. The first change occurred in the standards for nitrogen oxides, which EPA administrators concluded were not as extreme a problem as they had believed in the past. New methods for measuring concentrations in the air led to the discovery that only two of the forty-seven regions with nitrogen oxide levels exceeding the primary standards actually did so.[24] Although the standard (goal) has not been changed, the official perception of present nitrogen oxide concentrations in the air has been drastically altered.

The law also provides for courts to oversee the setting of such standards, and industries have filed suits challenging the standards set in almost every case. Some revision, stemming from these lawsuits, has already taken place. EPA changed its secondary standard for sulfur oxides in response to one such suit,[25] and many additional changes will ensue before we have any clear notion of the federal policy regarding ambient-air concentrations of even these six pollutants.

## IMPLEMENTATION: EFFLUENT AND EMISSION STANDARDS AT THE SOURCE

The establishment of ambient-air and water-quality standards, while attempting to define pollution, did not provide for the accomplishment of these goals. As we have seen in the case of state control programs, once environmental standards are set there are a number of other steps necessary before their attainment. If air and water quality are to reach the goals set for them by state or federal authorities, these standards must be linked to the actual amounts of wastes being discharged into air and water—the all-important emission standards. In 1965 state agencies were charged with the task of selecting the method for achieving water quality; each state was required to submit an implementation plan for review by federal officials in the same manner as they review the standards themselves. One innovative change made in the 1965 clean-water amendments, however, was an acceleration of the process of enforcement. The federal government now had authority to initiate court cases against individual polluters in the event that they violated the state-determined water-quality standards, thereby bypassing the time-consuming conference technique.

The 1970 amendments to the Clean Air Act met the problem of enforcement in two distinct ways. First, as in the water law, each state was required to submit an implementation plan for achieving actual ambient-air standards. The methods by which states were expected to achieve these goals included setting their own emission limitations for various pollutants, establishing schedules and timetables for compliance with such controls, and effecting changes in land-use patterns and transportation facilities. Individual state policy makers determined the exact mix of administrative methods by using their own discretion. It was thereby recognized that the varying degree to which different sources of emissions contribute to the pollution problem in state and local areas should be considered when determining how to achieve national ambient-air-quality standards.

Once again the process of obtaining federal approval of state action brought forth arguments over the wisdom of allowing states to plan to degrade their environment below the existing quality. This time the federal government leaned initially toward the direction of allowing the cleanest regions of the country to come down to the level to which the dirtiest were being asked to rise. Some state politicians and many environmentalists were adamant in their opposition to this stance. As it had done with other sticky problems concerning the environment, the Sierra Club took the problem to a federal court, which decided that EPA was *required* to reject any state implementation plan allowing for significant deterioration in air quality, even if it would still meet federal primary and secondary air-quality standards.[26]

The interpretation of "significant deterioration" remained in the balance and the administration's response to this unspoken question came in the form of EPA guidelines issued to the states in August 1974. States were informed that they might reclassify all their airsheds downward to the national standards because, in the words of John R. Quarles, Jr., administrator of EPA, "Deterioration of air quality can be regarded as 'significant' only within the broader perspective of public expectations and desires concerning the manner in which a particular region should be developed."[27] Whatever the states' response to his statement, it seemed certain that the Sierra Club would appeal to the courts once more.

The outcome of arguments over nondegradation statements aside, the plans formulated by the states were due in EPA in 1972, and by June 1973 EPA had fully approved fourteen plans and partially approved forty-one other plans, covering various segments of the states and including interstate regions.[28] Even after approval of such plans the legislation provides for a three-year time lag during which states may work to achieve primary air standards. No specified time frame is given for achieving the secondary standards, however, and in some cases states were given extensions for even the commencement of plan preparations.

The earliest date by which any state is required to achieve national primary ambient-air standards is 1975, and EPA can extend that deadline by two years. Just as it may replace unapproved state air- and water-quality standards, EPA is also empowered to draft its own implementation plan in substitution for an inadequate state plan. And, like the clean water amendments of 1965, the 1970 air law empowered EPA to take any violator of the states' implementation plans directly to court after thirty days' notice. If the administrator of EPA finds that violations of a state's implementation plan are widespread and interprets this as an unwillingness on the state's part to effectively administer its own program, he may take over the administration of the entire plan. Whether or not EPA will choose to utilize this discretionary power any more often than it did earlier powers remains to be seen.

Another crucial question—whether EPA would begin utilizing its power to litigate before the 1975 deadline for achieving federal primary ambient-air-quality standards had passed—has already been answered. Some court cases were filed in 1973 and one, against U.S. Steel plants in Gary, Indiana, was settled by agreement in September 1974,[29] but unless or until EPA's budget and personnel are greatly increased it seems unlikely to be able to launch a truly comprehensive enforcement effort throughout all fifty states. The federal government will continue to rely primarily on state enforcement efforts, with occasional prodding from the federal level as an incentive for the states to act.

The 1970 amendments, besides providing for state implementation plans, provide for another means of achieving the federally mandated ambient-air standards—the imposition of federally defined emission standards, the logical next step in federal assumption of enforcement powers. These emission standards were limited to new sources of air pollution and were designed to control only those pollutants that the administrator of EPA considered of sufficient importance to warrant federal standards. By mid-1973 standards had been created for four types of plants: fossil-fuel electric-generating plants, cement plants, and sulfuric- and nitric-acid-manufacturing plants. EPA has the authority to add other types of plants depending on the importance it places on these sources of pollutants. Emission standards are the product of EPA's determination of the best technologically feasible results, based on its knowledge of a given industry's capacity for pollution control. States had the option of incorporating into their own implementation plans a procedure for enforcing the federal standards of performance for new sources. If EPA decides that state procedures are sufficient it may turn over to them responsibility for administering the whole program; again, much policy depends on administrative discretion and intergovernmental bargaining.

One major method states have relied on to meet their federally mandated goals has been to set limits to the sulfur content of fuels used in electric-utility plants and heating plants. During the fuel shortage of 1973–74, however, EPA issued guidelines to the states most dependent on imported oil, recommending that they change these requirements to permit the use of higher-sulfur oil and to convert some plants from oil to coal. Because of the scarcity of clean fuels, EPA assumed the policy position that these supplies should be utilized primarily in areas of greatest need (highly polluted areas) and not in relatively clean regions. In June 1974 this attitude became official congressional policy with the passage of the Energy Supply and Environmental Coordinating Act. It directed EPA to review all states' implementation plans with an eye towards loosening controls on stationary sources of pollutants.[30] By early 1975 Ford administration spokesmen were proposing the postponement of meeting federal primary standards until the 1980s, and federal air-pollution policy was entering a markedly new period of reformulation.

## AUTO-EMISSION CONTROLS: POLICY REVISION

The decision to allow EPA to set new-source-emission standards for stationary air-pollution sources was not unprecedented, coming fully five years after the 1965 delegation of authority to the federal government for assuming control over motor vehicle emissions. The primary reason for this decision is self-evident: Mobile sources of pollution do not respond easily to control efforts by state and local governments, yet because they contribute so dramatically to the overall problem of air pollution some national abatement program was needed. What was uniquely new about auto-emission controls was not that the federal government set the goals but that the legislation turned over to EPA primary responsibility for enforcing the law instead of assigning this authority back to the states, as it did with stationary sources.

A "certification of conformity," which each automotive corporation was required to obtain for every model it produced, was the method of enforcement. A penalty of $10,000 accompanied each violation, which was defined as the sale of a motor vehicle or engine not covered by a certification. EPA was authorized to conduct tests or to contract for someone else to do so in order to insure that cars coming off the assembly line were indeed in conformity with the emission standards set; nevertheless, EPA itself estimated in 1973 that well over half the new vehicles in operation in the United States did not in fact meet the requirements under which they were supposedly manufactured.[31] This was attributed in part to improper maintenance by owners and to inadequate quality control by manufacturers. A large share of the blame necessarily fell on federal rules that permitted certification on the basis of a tiny percentage of cars coming off the assembly line. This situation was even more confused prior to 1972, when manufacturers were permitted to average the results of a number of emission tests.

Despite evident loopholes, auto-emission controls constituted the first and only congressional mandate to EPA to undertake directly enforcement of pollution controls without the assistance of state government. Proper maintenance, however, is crucial for the continuing effectiveness of control devices, and only state authorities are authorized to test vehicles after their initial sale and subsequent entry into the mainstream of traffic. Even so, most testing programs remain voluntary and vary radically from state to state.

Congressionally mandated auto-emission standards were initially set only for hydrocarbons and carbon monoxide and were first applied to the 1968 model year. No absolute limit for either of the pollutants was set; each standard was stated as a percentage emission reduction. In other words, a baseline of emissions was established based on the actual exhausts produced by cars without any controls. Percentage reductions in emissions of carbon monoxide and hydrocarbons were specified for the 1968 model cars. In 1970 Congress set new emission standards by amending the Clean Air Act. Under these amendments hydrocarbons and carbon monoxide were both to be reduced by ninety percent from emissions allowed for the 1970 car models. Nitrogen oxides were added to the list and a ninety-percent reduction of those emissions was prescribed based on 1971 emissions, when no standards for nitrogen oxides existed.[32]

The goals to reduce carbon monoxide and hydrocarbons by ninety percent were set for 1975 model cars; 1976 was the target date for reducing nitrogen emissions. Provision was made for reconsideration of these standards, and soon after it became possible to do so, car manufacturers began to petition for delay of the deadlines. During 1972 EPA officials managed to hold fast to the 1975 and 1976 deadlines because, they argued, sufficient lead time remained for the development of technology making the goal attainable. In April 1973, after a federal court ordered the administrator of EPA to reconsider his 1972 decision, EPA granted the one-year extension provided by the law, effectively postponing the 1975 standards until 1976.[33] Both the court and administrators made it clear that they were basing their policy change on economic grounds; potential job losses threatened by the automotive industry overrode whatever consideration they may have given to public-health hazards. EPA, by administrative fiat, also extended the 1976 deadline for nitrogen-oxide reduction to 1977.

Once the limits to administrative discretion written into the original law were reached, auto manufacturers turned their attention to altering the original legislation. Although EPA officials were reluctant to further weaken their stance toward auto emissions, the automotive and gasoline industries found other allies in the Nixon administration. Both the newly created Federal Energy Office and the Office of Management and Budget urged Congress to radically alter the Clean Air Act. Debate in Congress centered around such issues as the claim that emission-control devices reduce engine efficiency and therefore contribute to increased gasoline consumption and fuel shortages. Some industry and government scientists argued that health hazards from sulfates could prove worse than those now encountered by the public if cars were fitted with oxidation catalysts —the strategy devised for meeting the original 1975 standards. In effect, administration spokesmen urged that before any really stringent emission standards could be applied, industry must have more time to develop technologies for handling the same problems they had supposedly been working on since 1965 when the first law was passed.

In June 1974 Congress passed the Energy Supply and Environmental Coordination Act in response both to these pressures and to the gasoline shortage of the previous winter. Interim emission standards set by EPA for 1975, when the original statutory standards were postponed, were extended through 1976, and further discretionary power was written into the law to allow EPA to extend these standards one additional year.[34] National policy for a ninety-percent reduction of the three most important automotive pollutants by 1975 has already undergone considerable revision. All three branches of government have played a role in this revision of policy: courts, Congress, and above all, the executive branch. Strategies developed by other important actors outside official decision-making agencies—primarily gasoline and car producers—have contributed heavily to these recent decisions. More importantly, all indications are that federal air-quality policy will continue to be revised. Early in 1975 the Ford administration proposed an energy-conservation package that included an additional five-year extension of auto-emission standards, effectively postponing the original policy goal well into the 1980s.[35]

If the 1970 amendments to the Clean Air Act are interpreted as a response to demands made by antipollution forces, certainly developments since then must be interpreted as responses to the backlash created by this very policy. The attempt to control auto emissions is the most radical change in pollution-control efforts yet enacted in the United States for it is the one instance in which direct control was delegated to federal administrators. It represents a first response to the larger demand that total responsibility for environmental quality be shifted to the national level because of discontent with state and local programs of pollution control. The main argument in favor of federal control was that local and state officials often proved too responsive to private industrial demands on their policy making. Recent developments would seem to indicate, however, that national officials are not immune from such influences either, especially when the industry involved occupies a pivotal position in the national economy.

## POLLUTION-CONTROL TECHNOLOGY MANDATED

Setting emission/effluent standards is the next logical step beyond creating ambient-air- and water-quality goals. This type of regulation nevertheless leaves to the discharger considerable discretion concerning the type of technology to apply in order to achieve the prescribed level of cleanliness for his wastes. To go one step further in control, it is necessary to prescribe the type of technology to use. Building on the precedent of the 1970 air-act amendments, Congress opted for a combination of effluent standards and technology prescription in the 1972 amendments to the Water Pollution Control Act. This latest change in enforcement technique was motivated in part by dissatisfaction with the results of the water-quality-standards method and in part by administrative experience with the auto-emissions-control program in which government scientists played an increasing role in the development of technology.

The newest regulations are divided into two parts: the first deals with privately owned and the second with publicly owned effluent-treatment plants. The goals are also stated in stages, the final one aiming, in 1985, at the accomplishment of "complete treatment" of all wastes discharged into American waterways. Two intermediate goals are to be attained first. By July 1, 1977, all privately owned waste-treatment plants (industrial and commercial establishments that do not empty their wastes into municipal sewage systems) will be required to install the "best practicable control technology currently available as defined by the Administrator of EPA." By the same date, publicly owned plants must meet "effluent limitations based upon secondary treatment as defined by the Administrator." By July 1, 1983, these limits will be raised: for privately owned treatment plants to "the best available technology economically achievable for each category or class (defined by the kind of waste it is processing) which will result in reasonable further progress toward the national goal of eliminating the discharge of all pollutants"; and for publicly owned treatment plants, to "the best practicable waste treatment technology."[36]

In contrast to the auto-emission standards set by the Clean Air Act itself these legislated goals were loosely defined, with considerable discretion left to the administrator of EPA. He was charged with determining the chemical, physical, and biological properties of pollutants that have received secondary treatment and passing this information along to operators of public sewage-treatment plants. He may choose to set the traditional kinds of percentage-reduction effluent standards state officials have created in the past. EPA was also charged with defining the "best practical technology currently available" for private effluent discharges. This constitutes a complex task, given the plethora of exotic wastes produced by different industries. Consequently, EPA decided to contract out to private research organizations this responsibility for determining the types of treatment to be demanded from various industries.

EPA was not left uninstructed in the formulation of these standards. It was admonished to:

> . . . include consideration of the total cost of application of technology in relation to the effluent reduction benefits to be achieved from such application, and shall also take into account the age of equipment and facilities involved, the process employed, the engineering aspects of the application of various types of control techniques, process changes, non-water quality environmental impact (including energy requirements), and such other factors as the Administrator deems appropriate.[37]

The traditional political concern with economic contingencies persists in these qualifications. It has been restated using the current language of welfare economics—making benefits from certain actions commensurate with the costs of achieving them. The object of the law is, nevertheless, to balance the equity between those who would benefit from having the water cleaned up and those who will bear the costs, giving neither interest total consideration. The increasing demand for cleaner water is to be tempered by such other specific needs as society's growing energy requirements—a consideration that, we have seen, has already had considerable impact on air standards.

Regardless of the type and level of treatment finally set by EPA, the crucial question remains: What provisions exist for enforcing the effluent/technology standards? Most waste treatment plants, that is, all those in existence prior to 1974, have until mid-1977 to comply with the first phase, and all have until 1983 to reach the second set of standards, but what means have been established for the attainment of these goals? Analogous to the case of stationary sources of air pollutants, the newest water-pollution law implies strongly that the first line of defense against violation of federal edicts will again be state agencies.

For the first time, a federally mandated permit system covers both public and private effluents, but the states are encouraged to develop or strengthen their own permit programs in order to carry out the federal law. The administrator of EPA is instructed to approve the permit program submitted by each state, provided that the state agency has the power to withdraw permits, reviews permits periodically for performance and does not simply issue pro forma permits that extend into the indefinite future, includes the public in its deliberations over permit requests and renewals, and keeps federal officials informed about the status of its permit program.

As in the Clean Air Act, if the administrator of EPA decides that a given state is not administering its program in conformity with federal regulations he may withdraw approval of such a program. Just as there once existed the possibility of EPA's substituting its own water-quality standards for inadequate state standards, so there now exists the possibility of a federal permit system. In order to make this option a reality, however, EPA will have to assert its power.

Water-quality standards also continue to exist under the new law, but their role has been reduced to a supplementary function to be used in conjunction with the new effluent-technology standards. The law explicitly states that water-quality standards already approved by EPA for interstate waters will be retained; states should also set intrastate water standards or face the possibility of having EPA establish or change them if they do not meet EPA's approval. States must review and update their standards at least once every three years. In the future, however, it would seem that the usefulness of such water-quality standards will be restricted to those instances in which the effluent-technology standards established by the federal government are not strict enough to achieve the desired water quality. In other words, in those cases in which numerous waste dischargers are reducing their waste loads to the degree required by the "best practicable technology" without achieving the water-quality standards set for the receiving waters a higher effluent standard or additional technology other than that stipulated by federal regulation can be required. How often such an event will occur depends, of course, on the strictness of water-quality standards set for individual rivers.

What changes in behavior can be anticipated from the new amendments to the Federal Water Pollution Control Act? Builders of *new* public and private treatment plants are encouraged to anticipate enforcement efforts by building into their plans sufficient capacity to meet these new regulations; the law promises immunity from more stringent standards of performance during a ten-year period to any new plant operator, provided that the plant meet federal effluent standards at the time of its completion. Conceivably, owners of older waste-discharging plants might also begin upgrading their own facilities in anticipation of the 1977 and 1983 deadlines. More likely, if past behavior is any indicator, such waste dischargers will wait until a state agency puts pressure on them to comply with the effluent standards. The attitude of state officials toward this part of the law will depend to a large degree on the seriousness with which EPA personnel view their own authority to take a hard look at states' permit-issuing programs in light of the stated goals for 1977 and 1983.

The effectiveness of these programs must depend in part on the degree of cooperation between the state and federal levels of government. As we have already seen, funds promised in the 1972 legislation for municipal treatment plants have not been forthcoming from Washington. These funds undoubtedly played a large role in all states' plans for their public facilities. If they do not receive the promised grants-in-aid, most states will probably be unable to achieve the goals set. A recent government report mentioned that the level of federal funding for basic research into water-pollution problems makes it unlikely that the final 1985 goal will ever be reached.[38] The state of technology for treating water borne wastes will be so underdeveloped by 1985 that the "best practical" or even "best available" technology will still produce an effluent far from the "no discharge" goal stated in the law. In effect, a policy goal set by Congress in 1972, which appeared to be a considerable victory for antipollution groups, is rapidly becoming purely symbolic. The policy has been changed by decisions both of the executive branch and of individual state governments. Unless there is renewed interest generated at all levels of government all three deadlines may come and go without much measurable improvement in water quality.

## IMPACT OF FEDERAL WATER-QUALITY LAWS: THE CASE OF RESERVE MINING

Federally mandated technology is only the latest of many techniques by which the federal government has attempted to improve the quality of water in the United States. Few people would expect the 1972 amendments to have much impact before the 1980s, perhaps not even by the 1990s. Other federal enforcement programs have been in effect longer, but their histories are complex and often confusing. One famous case involving the Reserve Mining Company of Silver Bay, Minnesota illustrates what in fact happened during many of the stages through which the national enforcement effort has passed. A brief look at this history may give some indication as to why many proponents of pollution control felt additional efforts were needed.

Ironically it was in 1948, the year of the first Water Pollution Control Act, that Reserve Mining obtained its permit to dump tailings (wastes) into Lake Superior from the U.S. Army Corps of Engineers.[39] Although the 1899 permit requirement had not been observed by most industries, the size of the proposed operation and the site of the discharge made such a request necessary. The Corps has been unusually conscientious about keeping the Great Lakes free from navigational impediments and it has traditionally granted permits for dredging harbor facilities there and dumping the dredgings farther out into the lakes. Because of the size of Reserve's operation and the fact that its chutes empty directly into the lake at the shoreline, it was considered necessary to apply for a permit, which was granted without incident.

During the 1940s many of the high-grade iron ore fields in the upper Middle West had become played out, and the steel industry was progressively turning to alternative sources of raw material. One such source, found in abundant supply in the Mesabi Range of northern Minnesota, is taconite ore, an inferior grade of ore that contains some iron together with varying amounts of nickel, copper, zinc, lead, chromium, phosphorus, manganese, silica and arsenic. Usable iron can be extracted from the rock through the use of enormous quantities of water and the production of equally significant amounts of wastes. Two of the giants of the steel industry, Republic Steel and Armco Steel, banded together to form a subsidiary, the Reserve Mining Company, whose task it is to utilize the bountiful taconite deposits and produce the iron pellets needed to keep the parent companies' steel mills running.[40] By 1955, when the company reached full operation, it was daily distributing some 67,000 tons of mineral wastes into Lake Superior. This practice was to continue through twenty years of increasing federal involvement in water-pollution-control work.

During the first decade of Reserve's operations, the federal water-pollution-abatement program, as previously indicated, consisted of two distinct functions: research and development, and enforcement through conferences. Both functions affected Reserve Mining but neither produced any change in its behavior. Ironically, many politicians who are most active in establishing government regulatory programs to protect the public safety are equally eager to protect their local constituents from the effects of the very legislation they sponsor. In this respect Reserve Mining had one of the most powerful protectors of all—Representative John Blatnik of Minnesota, for many years chairman of the Rivers and Harbors Subcommittee of the House Public Works Committee, who drafted and sponsored many water-pollution-control bills. One of the benefits of being chairman of a key committee in any field is the ability to obtain for one's district some of the federal largesse involved in the program. This largesse came in the form of a National Water Quality Laboratory that opened in Duluth, Minnesota in 1965, ten years after the initial legislation authorizing such facilities was drafted by Blatnik's committee.

Touted by Blatnik as "a watchful, protective beacon to preserve Lake Superior,"[41] it was in danger of living up to its title shortly after its opening. An employee of the laboratory, an aquatic biologist named Dr. Louis Williams, initiated studies into the quality of Lake Superior water and began making speeches and writing articles about the effect of taconite tailings on this quality. He warned that Reserve's discharges were increasing the trace-metal content of the lake and stimulating algae growths that might eventually lead to eutrophication of the lake.[42] His superiors, both in Duluth and in the Washington, D.C. headquarters of the Federal Water Pollution Control Administration, ridiculed his stories of danger to the lake. By August 1967 Dr. Williams had been "persuaded" to return to academic life far from Minnesota.[43]

This did not satisfy all interested parties, however. If it is the function of otherwise conservation-minded congressmen to protect the worst polluters (read, important employers) in their districts, it is also the function of politicians who represent constituents injured, but not benefited by polluters, to draw attention to polluters' offenses. Senator Gaylord Nelson of Wisconsin, a near neighbor of Reserve Mining, early assumed this role. Unencumbered by Representative Blatnik's economic and political problems, Nelson argued that Reserve Mining was polluting Lake Superior. He was joined by other Wisconsin politicians, as well as by many Minnesota-based conservation groups such as the Minnesota Environmental Control Citizens Association (MECCA), the Save Lake Superior Association, and Clean Air Clear Water Unlimited.[43] Under their urging the FWPCA regional office in 1967 took up officially where Dr. Williams had left off. Given the fate of Dr. Williams and the fact that Charles Stoddard, the chief investigator, was a former associate of Representative Blatnik, the results of this study were somewhat unexpected. It concluded that, despite Reserve's claim that its wastes were lying inert at the bottom of the lake, in fact some 5,000 tons of the daily deposit had been so finely ground that they had remained in suspension for an indefinite period and were contributing to the eutrophication of the lake. The report, completed at the end of 1968, recommended that Reserve Mining be given three years to find another dumping site for its wastes.[44]

Reactions to this report were immediate and predictable. Reserve's representatives immediately put pressure on the secretary of the interior, Stewart Udall, to supress and discredit the report. Senator Nelson and his associates stepped up their attempts to have a federal conference convened on the problems of Lake Superior. The power to convene such conferences had existed since 1956, and as early as 1963 in a hearing before the Senate Air and Water Pollution Subcommittee, Senator Nelson had suggested the need for such a conference on Lake Superior. He was overridden by Murray Stein, the chief enforcement officer of FWPCA, on the ground that the problem, if indeed one existed, was a purely intrastate one, and at the moment Minnesota's pollution-control agency seemed uninterested in its remedy.[45] The Stoddard Report, however, gave new ammunition to the proponents of a conference, and Secretary Udall signed the papers unilaterally initiating a conference over the objections of Minnesota.

The invocation of the one available federal method of enforcement had taken over ten years, from 1957 when the first water-pollution-control conference opened, to May 13, 1969 when the Lake Superior Conference convened in Duluth. The results seemed hardly worth the effort. Throughout the conference Reserve Mining's lawyers and chemists and Minnesota's Pollution Control Agency debunked the seriousness of the situation. Since the findings of the conference required unanimous agreement, the only recommendation made was that Reserve's wastes be kept "under continuing surveillance."[46] The consensus seemed to be that Reserve's scientists had bested both FWPCA people and the representatives of Michigan and Wisconsin by arguing that any pollution that did exist had not been proven beyond a reasonable doubt to extend beyond Minnesota's boundaries. Even though the conference was reconvened both in 1970 and 1971 and other polluters were assigned a cleanup deadline to meet, Reserve Mining was never given such a deadline.

## RESERVE MINING IN COURT

By 1971, however, a new era in federal water-pollution-enforcement policy seemed to be emerging. Emphasis was removed from the conference technique and placed instead on water-quality standards set by each state according to the 1965 clean-water amendments. In 1969 Minnesota had submitted its standards and had them approved by the federal agency. By 1971 EPA administrators were beginning to take seriously the authority given them in the 1965 law to take individual polluters directly to court. In 1972 EPA filed notice with Reserve Mining that it was about to initiate a federal suit against Reserve with the acquiescence of Minnesota.[47] Changes at the federal level paralleled changes in Minnesota's politics and a new governor showed signs of being more responsive to demands from antipollution groups in his state.[48] By August 73 when the trial began in the Federal District Court in Duluth, the state of Minnesota and the Minnesota Pollution Control Agency had joined the suit filed by EPA.[49]

These changes in the attitudes of enforcement officials at both the state and federal levels were in part the result of subtle political shifts. Opinion changes had been taking place gradually since the first complaints were made against Reserve by a minority of ecologists in the late 1950s. Changes in attitudes were also due to alarming new developments within the scientific community. For many years a controversy paralleling water pollution has raged in the field of industrial health and safety of workers in the asbestos industry. Expert opinion on this subject varies, of course. Industrial chemists and biologists are as reluctant to consider injury done to industrial workers from exposure to asbestos as Reserve's experts are to discuss pollution. But some government scientists and union spokesmen are convinced of the danger from exposure to asbestos by the higher rate of mortality from cancer, asbestosis, and mesothelioma among asbestos workers, compared with the general population.[50] It is now apparent that Reserve's daily 67,000 tons of discharge contain not only the normal pollutants but also minute amphibole fibers, many of which are chemically identical to amosite asbestos. Recent analyses of Lake Superior water show a high concentration of these minute amphibole fibers.[51]

By the time the case reached the courtroom of Judge Miles Lord in August 1973 the primary argument centered around the issue of the hundreds of thousands of residents both in Wisconsin and Minnesota who draw their water supplies from Lake Superior and who were thus continually exposed to amphibole fibers. By February 1973 Judge Lord was sufficiently convinced of the urgency of the matter to push the mining company representatives toward the development of alternative methods of waste disposal on land. Instead of taking the hint Reserve Mining and its parent companies responded with a wide variety of delaying tactics.

First, they argued that Armco and Republic Steel were not responsible, as Reserve Mining was the only wrongdoer. Since Reserve makes no profits, it could hardly be expected to expend monies on a cleanup process nor could it even pay any fines levied against it. Considerable time and effort were devoted to demonstrating that Reserve is not an autonomous corporation, that its decisions are made by Armco and Republic, that it makes no profit, that it turns over its total production of iron pellets to its two parent bodies, and that it receives only compensation for expenses. After months of argument Armco and Republic were joined to the suit.[52]

Second, industrial attorneys argued that their employers' engineering staffs lacked the expertise to prepare an on-land disposal system. Only after governmental and Environmental Defense Fund experts made their own technical suggestions through the judge would the industrial experts admit the feasibility of the operation; however, after some months of discovery hearings, it was found that the mining company had had secret engineering studies made into the technical aspects of the problem months before the trial began.[53]

Third, Reserve Mining argued that it could not afford to make the necessary adjustments and that if it were forced to do so it would need federal assistance. The judge, after investigating the corporate profits of the two parent companies, concluded that "This is not an occasion that calls for massive public aid to a dying industry, since Republic and Armco are two of the largest and most profitable corporations in the country."[54] Finally it was argued that the residents of such towns as Silver Bay and Beaver Bay, Minnesota, both of which had joined the suit on the company's side, would be thrown out of work if the company were made to provide an on-land disposal system.[55]

During a nine-month trial conflicting testimony was taken from more than one hundred expert witnesses representing all sides of the controversy, from chemists and medical doctors employed by Reserve Mining to those sent to intervene in the case by the Environmental Defense Fund. On April 20, 1974, Judge Lord concluded that prolonged exposure to asbestos particles "can produce asbestosis, mesothelioma, and cancer of the lung, gastrointestinal tract and larynx."[56] He also ruled that the daily discharge of the 67,000 tons of tailings constituted a violation of the water-quality standards ratified by the EPA in 1969, and that, in addition, it constituted a violation of Minnesota law. As for the economic arguments, he concluded:

> If in fact the people of Silver Bay were the only ones exposed to the health risk there might be some weight to be given their conscious choice to take the associated risk involved to continue at their jobs. Even then, however, the Court would have to take a broader view of the matter. In the first place, the Court would be concerned

> with those who were unable to make a real choice, particularly the children who must abide by the choice made by their parents. Secondly, this Court would have to answer the question, "can this Court permit a commercial industry to require its work force to make such a choice to endanger their lives, and the lives of their families when in fact the commercial industry has the economic and technological means to eliminate any real health risk?" Consistent with governmental regulation of industrial safety and health conditions, the obvious answer is NO.[57]

On that day, he ordered a shutdown of Reserve Mining until such time as its corporate decision makers could discover a way to provide for on-land disposal of the tailings.

Two days later, the Circuit Court of Appeals overruled that decision, ordered the plant reopened, and sent the case back to Judge Lord for further consideration.[58] Since that time, the companies involved have made suggestions for on-land disposal sites, all of which have proved unacceptable to both Minnesota and EPA representatives. Eventually some compromise will be worked out whereby the company will undertake to develop such a site over a three- to five-year time period. In the meantime 67,000 tons of filings continue to be dumped daily.

Throughout the trial, experts disagreed on the degree of proof needed to link asbestos waste with cancer, an argument of several years' standing among experts on industrial safety. No conclusions acceptable to all have been reached, and many scientists believe that considerable time will have to elapse before the long-term effects on human beings of exposure to asbestos particles will be scientifically demonstrable. Perhaps twenty years from now a scientific comparison will be made between the numbers of Duluth residents who succumb to gastrointestional cancer and a control group drawn from the rest of the country. At that time a statistically accurate statement of the increased risk from exposure to asbestos will be known. One segment of the population will no doubt await the results of such a study with impatience—residents of Duluth and other towns who use Lake Superior water for all their cooking, washing, bathing, and drinking needs.

## SUMMARY

Federal legislation in the field of pollution control began slowly and increased incrementally over the years following the 1940s. Originally, federal legislation was restricted to research and development—a program usually accepted by other levels of government without controversy. Solid-waste management is at this stage today. Subsequent grants-in-aid for water-and air-pollution control were provided, including grants to state enforcement agencies. Under pressure from environmentalists, the federal government eventually entered the enforcement field, starting with the conference technique—attempting to get state agencies voluntarily to assume responsibility for implementation of mutually defined goals for pollution control.

When this proved unsatisfactory, federal power was gradually increased. First, the authority to oversee the setting of ambient-air and water-quality standards was created, with the possibility for federally imposed standards. Goals in the form of water and air standards can have little effect without effluent/emission standards. This important aspect of pollution control was left to the states until 1970 for stationary air-pollution sources and 1972 for water sources. Starting in 1968 the federal government initiated emission standards for mobile sources of air pollutants. These standards were gradually strengthened at first, but recently this trend has been reversed, and federal resolve concerning stationary sources seems to have diminished as well. At the present time, rather ambitious goals for air and water quality are symbolically spelled out in federal legislation, but practical possibilities for achieving these goals remain uncertain. There is still a mixed strategy of reliance on state and federal enforcement agencies and techniques. In the past environmentalists have considered federal officials to be their most consistent ally, but recently reasons have appeared for reconsidering that evaluation.

## NOTES

1. 33 U.S. Code 407 (1971)
2. Executive Order No. 11574, December 23, 1970, 35 Federal Register 1972.
3. Kalur v. Resor, 335 Federal Supplement 1 (1971).
4. Public Law 92–500, 402(a) (4) and (5) states that: All permits for discharges into the navigable water issued pursuant to Section 13 of the Act of March 1899, shall be deemed to be permits issued under this title, and . . .
5. Public Law 80–845.
6. The Federal Air Pollution Control Act is codified at 42 U.S. Code 1857. It was amended in 1963, 1965, 1967, and 1970.
7. The Federal Water Pollution Control Act is codified at 33 U.S. Code 466. It was amended in 1956, 1961, 1965, 1966, 1970, and 1972.
8. 33 U.S. Code 466, 1 (b) 1973.
9. 42 U.S. Code 1857, 101 (a) (3) 1973.
10. Council on Environmental Quality, *Fourth Annual Report: Environmental Quality* (Washington, D.C.: U.S. Government Printing Office, 1973), p. 203.

11. *New York Times*, January 30, 1971, p. 1

12. *New York Times*, January 11, 1974, p. 1.

13. U.S. General Accounting Office, *Examination into the Effectiveness of the Construction Grant Program for Abating, Controlling, and Preventing Water Pollution* (Washington, D.C.: U.S. Government Printing Office, 1969).

14. Public Law 80–845, 3 (d) (2).

15. From unpublished data of EPA. Each conference is available in the form of transcribed proceedings from EPA.

16. See, for example, U.S. Department of the Interior, Federal Water Pollution Control Administration, *Conference in the Matter of Pollution of Lake Michigan and Its Tributary Basin*, 1968.

17. From unpublished data of EPA.

18. U.S. Department of the Interior, Federal Water Pollution Control Administration, *Conference in the Matter of Pollution of the Navigable Waters of Puget Sound*, 3, (1967), p. 26

19. Murrary Stein, "The Actual Operation of the Federal Water Pollution Control Administration," *Natural Resources Lawyer*, 3 (1970): 41, 46.

20. From the author's personal observations of the conference on Lake Michigan held in Chicago in May 1970.

21. From unpublished data of EPA.

22. U.S. Department of the Interior, Federal Water Pollution Control Act., *Water Quality Standards Conference for the State of Iowa*, 1969.

23. 36 Federal Register 8186 (1971).

24. Council on Environmental Quality, *Fourth Annual Report*, 1973, p. 166.

25. Kennecott Copper Corporation v. EPA, 462 Federal 2d 846.

26. Sierra Club v. Ruckelshaus, 344 Federal Supplement 253. Affirmed by U.S. Supreme Court tie vote, 41 *U.S. Law Week*, p. 4825.

27. *New York Times*, August 17, 1974, p. 1.

28. Council on Environmental Quality, op. cit., p. 157.

29. *Chicago Tribune*, September 12, 1974, p. 6.

30. Public Law 93–319.

31. Council on Environmental Quality, op. cit., p. 156.

32. Public Law 91–604, 84 Stat. 1676 (1970).

33. Council on Environmental Quality, op. cit., p. 163.

34. Public Law 93–319, Section 5. Council on Environmental Quality, *Fifth Annual Report*, p. 128.

35. *New York Times*, January 22, 1974, p. 1.

36. Public Law 92–500, 301 (b) (1) and (2).

37. Public Law 92–500 304 (b) (1) (B).

38. U.S. General Accounting Office, *Research and Demonstration Programs to Achieve Water Quality Goals*, 1974.

39. David Zwick and Marcy Benstock, *Water Wasteland* (New York: Grossman, 1971), p.142.

40. Ibid.

41. Zwick and Benstock, op. cit., p. 156.

42. Ibid.

43. Zwick and Benstock, op. cit., p. 153.

44. "Environmental Impact of Taconite Waste Disposal on Lake Superior," unpublished report on file with EPA in Washington, D.C.

45. U.S. Congress, Senate, "Hearings before a Special Subcommittee of Air and Water Pollution of the Committee on Public Works," 88th Congress, 1st sess., June 17, 1963, p. 55.

46. U.S. Department of the Interior, Federal Water Pollution Control Act, *Proceeding: Conference on Pollution of Lake Superior and Its Tributary Basin, Minnesota-Wisconsin-Michigan,* May 13–15, 1969.

47. United States v. Reserve Mining, 6 ERC 1659.

48. Zwick and Benstock, op. cit., p. 153.

49. United States v. Reserve Mining, 6 ERC 1658.

50. Paul Brodeur, "Annals of Industry—Casualties of the Workplace," *The New Yorker* (November 5, 1973): 92–142; (November 12, 1973): 85–150; (November 19, 1973): 87–149.

51. United States v. Reserve Mining, 6 ERC 1449.

52. Id. at 1662.

53. Id. at 1692.

54. Id. at 1452.

55. Id. at 1658.

56. Id. at 1449.

57. Id. at 1693.

58. *New York Times,* April 23, 1974, p.1.

## BIBLIOGRAPHY: PART 2

### Books

Anderson, Walt, ed. *Politics and Environment*. Pacific Palisades, Calif.: Goodyear, 1970.

Aylesworth, T. G. *This Vital Air, This Vital Water*. Chicago: Rand McNally, 1968.

Bernarde, Melvin A. *Our Precarious Habitat*. New York: W. W. Norton, 1970.

Brady, Nyle C., ed. *Agriculture and the Quality of Our Environment*. Washington, D.C.: American Association for the Advancement of Science, 1967.

Breman, J. *The Pollution Paradox*. New York: Spartan Books, 1966.

Briggs, Peter. *Water, the Vital Essence*. New York: Harper & Row, 1967.

Battan, Louis J. *The Unclean Sky*. Garden City, N.Y.: Anchor Books, 1966.

Caldwell, Lynton Keith. *Environment: A Challenge to Modern Society*. Garden City, N.Y.: Anchor Books, 1971.

———. *Environmental Studies*. Bloomington, Ind.: Institute of Public Administration, 1967.

Camp, Thomas R. *Water and Its Impurities*. New York: Reinhold, 1963.

Carr, Donald E. *The Breath of Life*. New York: Berkeley, 1970.

———. *Death of the Sweet Waters*. New York: Berkeley, 1965.

Crenson, Matthew A. *The Un-Politics of Air Pollution*. Baltimore: Johns Hopkins Univ. Press, 1971.

Davies, J. Clarence, III. *The Politics of Pollution*. New York: Pegasus, 1970.

DeBell, Garrett. *The Environmental Handbook*. New York: Ballantine Books, 1970.

Devos, Anthony; Pearson, Norman; Silveston, P. S.; and Dryman, W. R. *The Pollution Reader*. Montreal: Harvest House, 1968.

Dohm, R. R. *Politics and Pollution: Defeat of 1961 Proposition for Metropolitan Sanitary District for Minneapolis-St. Paul*. Minneapolis: Univ. of Minnesota Press, 1965.

Edmunds, Stahrl, and Letey, John. *Environmental Administration*. New York: McGraw-Hill, 1973.

Esposito, John C. *Vanishing Air*. New York: Grossman, 1970.

Fadiman, Clifton, and White, Jean, eds. *Ecocide . . . and Thoughts Toward Survival*. Palo Alto, Calif: James E. Freel, 1971.

Falk, Richard A. *This Endangered Planet*. New York: Random, 1971.

Flack, J. Ernest, and Shipley, Margaret C. *Man and the Quality of His Environment*. Boulder, Colorado: Univ. of Colorado Press, 1967.

Goldman, Marshall I., ed. *Ecology and Economics: Controlling Pollution in the 1970s*. Englewood Cliffs, N.J.: Prentice-Hall, 1972.

Graham, Frank, Jr. *Disaster by Default.* New York: Modern Literary Editions, 1966.

Henning, Daniel H. *Environmental Policy and Administration.* New York: American Elsevier, 1974.

Jamison, Egbert, and Adams, Francis, eds. *Municipal Code of Chicago for 1881.* Chicago: Bearch, Bernard, 1881.

Johnson, Huey D., ed. *No Deposit—No Return.* Menlo Park, Calif.: Addison-Wesley, 1970.

Klein, Louis. *River Pollution.* London: Butterworths, 1966.

Murphy, Earl Finbar. *Man and His Environment.* New York: Harper & Row, 1971.

———. *Water Purity.* Madison: Univ. of Wisconsin Press, 1961.

National Research Council. *Waste Management and Control.* Washington: National Academy of Science, 1966.

Paulsen, David F., and Denhardt, Robert B., eds. *Pollution and Public Policy.* New York: Dodd, Mead, 1973.

Revelle, Roger, and Landsberg, Hans H., eds. *America's Changing Environment.* Boston: Houghton Mifflin, 1970.

Ridgeway, James. *The Politics of Ecology.* New York: E. P. Dutton, 1970.

Roos, Leslie L., Jr. *The Politics of Ecosuicide.* New York: Holt, Rinehart and Winston, 1971.

Rosenbaum, Walter A. *The Politics of Environmental Concern.* New York: Praeger, 1973.

Schadter, Ester R. *Enforcing Air Pollution Controls: Case Study of New York City.* New York: Praeger, 1974.

Small, William E. *The Third Pollution: The National Problem of Solid Waste Disposal.* New York: Praeger, 1971.

Smith, Grahame J. C.; Steck, Henry J.; and Surette, Gerald. *Our Ecological Crisis: Its Biological, Economic and Political Dimensions.* New York: Macmillan, 1974.

Stepp, James M., and Macaulay, H. H. *The Pollution Problem.* Washington: American Enterprise Institute for Public Policy Research, 1968.

Tsuru, Shigeto, ed. *Environmental Disruption.* Tokyo: Proceedings of International Symposium, 1970.

Willrich, Ted L., and Hines, N. William. *Water Pollution Control and Abatement.* Ames, Iowa: Iowa State Univ. Press, 1965.

Zwick, David, and Benstock, Marcy. *Water Wasteland.* New York: Grossman, 1971.

## Government Documents

*Federal Register*

42 U.S. Code 1857 et seq. *Clean Air Act,* as Amended.

33 U.S. Code 407 et seq. *Rivers and Harbors Act,* as Amended.

33 U.S. Code 1251 et seq. *Federal Water Pollution Control Act,* as Amended.

Public Law 89–272, as Amended by Public Law 91–512. *Resource Recovery Act*, as Amended.

Public Law 91–604. *Clean Air Act*, 1970.

Public Law 92–500. *Clean Water Act*, 1972.

U.S. Comptroller General. General Accounting Office. *Examination into the Effectiveness of the Construction Grant Program for Abating, Controlling and Preventing Water Pollution*, 1969.

———. *Research and Demonstration Programs to Achieve Water Quality Goals*, 1974.

U.S. Council on Environmental Quality. *First Annual Report*. Washington, D.C.: U.S. Government Printing Office, 1970.

———. *Second Annual Report*. Washington, D.C.: U.S. Government Printing Office, 1971.

———. *Third Annual Report*. Washington, D.C.: U.S. Government Printing Office, 1972.

———. *Fourth Annual Report*. Washington, D.C.: U.S. Government Printing Office, 1973.

———. *Fifth Annual Report*. Washington, D.C.: U.S. Government Printing Office, 1974.

U.S. Department of Health, Education and Welfare. *Proceedings: Conference on Water Pollution*, 1961.

———. *Proceedings: Conference into the Matter of Pollution of the Grand Calumet River*, 1965.

———. *Proceedings: Conference into the Matter of Pollution of Puget Sound*, 1962.

———. *Proceedings: Conference into the Matter of Pollution of the Mahoning River*, 1965.

———. *Proceedings: Conference into the Matter of Pollution of the Colorado Rivers*, 1970.

U.S. Department of the Interior, Federal Water Pollution Control Administration. *Proceedings: Conference into Pollution of the Chattahoochee River*, 1966.

———. *Proceedings: Conference into Pollution of Lake Tahoe*, 1967.

———. *Proceedings: Conference into Pollution of the Mississippi River*, 1967.

———. *Proceedings: Conference into Pollution of Lake Erie*, 1968.

———. *Proceedings: Conference on Pollution of Lake Superior and Its Tributary Basin—Minnesota-Wisconsin-Michigan*, 1969.

———. *Proceedings: Conference on Pollution of Lake Michigan and Its Tributary Basin*, 1968.

———. *Proceedings: Conference on the Matter of Pollution of the Navigable Waters of Puget Sound*, 3 vols., 1967.

———. *Water Quality Standards Conference for the State of Iowa*, 1969.

———. *Digest of FY 1970 State Program Plans.*

U.S. Environmental Protection Agency. *Digest of FY 1970 State Program Plans for Water Pollution Control.*

———. *Digest of FY 1971 State Program Plans for Water Pollution Control.*

———. *Digest of FY 1972 State Program Plans for Water Pollution Control.*

———. *Digest of FY 1973 State Program Plans for Water Pollution Control.*

———. *Digest of FY 1972 State Air Programs.*

———. *The Economics of Clean Water*. 2 vols., 1972.

———. *Enforcement Economics in Air Pollution Control*, 1973.

———. *Managing the Environment*, 1973.

———. *Monitoring and Air Quality Trends Report*, 1973.

———. *National Public Hearings on Power Plant Compliance with Sulfur Oxide Air Pollution Regulations*, 1974.

———. *National Strategy for Control of Sulfur Oxides from Electric Power Plants*, 1974.

———. *National Water Quality Inventory*, 2 vols., 1974.

———. *The Quality of Life Concept*, 1973.

U.S. Congress, Senate, Committee on Public Works. *A Study of Pollution—Water*. A staff report, 88th Congress, 1st sess., 1963.

U.S. Congress, Senate, Committee on Public Works. *A Study of Pollution—Air*, 88th Congress, 1st sess., 1963.

U.S. Congress, Senate, Committee on Public Works. *Hearings before a Special Subcommittee on Air and Water Pollution.* Committee on Public Works, Clean Air, 88th Congress, 1st sess., 1963.

U.S. Congress, Senate, Committee on Public Works. *Hearings on Thermal Pollution*, 90th Congress, 1st sess., 1968.

U.S. Congress, Senate, Committee on Public Works. *Progress in the Prevention and Control of Air Pollution*, 90th Congress, 2d sess., 1968.

U.S. Congress, Senate, Committee on Public Works. *Report from the National Academy of Sciences*, 93rd Congress, 2d sess., 1974.

U.S. Congress, Senate, Committee on Public Works. *Environmental Impact Statements*, 93rd Congress, 2d sess., 1974.

U.S. Congress. Senate. Committee on Public Works. *Air Quality and Automobile Emission Control.* 3 vols., 93rd Congress, 2d sess., 1974.

U.S. Congress, House, Committee on Government Operations. *Effects of Population Growth on Natural Resources and the Environment*, 91st Congress, 1st sess., 1969.

U.S. Congress, House, Committee on Government Operations. *The Environmental Decade*, 91st Congress, 2d sess., 1970.

U.S. Congress, House, Committee on Government Operations. *The Establishment of a National Industrial Wastes Inventory*, 91st Congress, 2d sess., 1970.

U.S. Congress, House, Committee on Public Works. *Hearings to Amend the Federal Water Pollution Control Act*, 87th Congress, 1st sess., 1961.

U.S. Congress, House, Committee on Public Works. *Hearings on the Federal Water Pollution Control Act Amendments*, 91st Congress, 1st sess., 1969.

U.S. Congress, House, Committee on Public Works. *Implementation of the Federal Water Pollution Control Act*, 93rd Congress, 1st sess., 1973.

U.S. Congress, House, Committee on Science and Astronautics. *The Adequacy of Technology for Pollution Abatement*, Serial Q, 1966.

U.S. Congress, Joint Economic Committee. *Economic Analysis and the Efficiency of Government, Part 6—Economic Incentives to Control Pollution*, 92nd Congress, 1st sess., 1971.

PART 3

# Current Questions Of Policy

CHAPTER SIX

# Causes of Pollution: Rival Hypotheses

The consensus among most U.S. public-policy makers is that a pollution problem exists, but this consensus does not extend to a plan for its solution. Differences of opinion over definition of the problem and identification of its causes are the primary stumbling blocks. Despite lack of agreement, however, there is no scarcity of possible definitions and causes from which to choose. Before policy makers can hope to reach a consensus for remedying the situation it is crucial that they first agree about how to define the problems and who should have this responsibility.

One example of consensus that exists among many Americans is our irritation at seeing discarded beverage containers alongside most roads in this country. The remedies that we prescribe vary radically, depending on the way we perceive the problem and assess the cause. Some define the problem as one of misplaced matter and the cause as careless and irresponsible people. Their solution, therefore, is simply to prevent individuals from disposing of their litter in this manner. "People start pollution; people can stop it," is the motto that best expresses this analysis of the situation. One method of achieving the goal of cleaner highways is to remind people of the antisocial nature of their behavior. The aluminum-container industry dumps this responsibility squarely on the consumer's conscience by imprinting its product with the message: "Dispose of properly" or "Do not litter." Others who share this interpretation of the problem recognize that the likelihood of a potential litterbug's heeding such a message is approximately that of an inveterate smoker's changing his habits because of the warning printed on his cigarette pack. They recommend other measures to achieve the same objective: stiffer fines for littering and more stringent enforcement of present laws by the state highway patrol.

Others, equally chagrined at the condition of the highways, perceive the problem differently and interpret it more broadly.

Consequently, their assessment of causation and suggestions for solutions are much different. They view discarded beer and soft drink cans not simply as a problem of poor distribution but also as one of oversupply. Most would agree that putting a stop to the American habit of hurling cans from cars would be beneficial for the landscape and would develop a sense of responsibility among the citizenry. However, to this school of thought, litter along the roads is only a symptom of a greater problem: the overabundance of disposable products of all kinds. Cajoling or coercing people into keeping these products inside their cars or even into depositing them into litter baskets leaves unsolved the more important problem of finding sufficient landfill space for a final resting place. In fact, the continued burial of flip-top cans is seen as one aspect of the biggest problem of all: *expending finite resources on disposable products*. Individuals and corporations who set priorities for use of scarce resources are considered the real culprits, not the actual can flinger. Solutions suggested by people who view the problem from this perspective are much different. They emphasize recycling resources rather than continuing their misuse in a flow-through economy. Methods for achieving recycling vary also from new, sophisticated technology for separating metals from other trash to banning the sale of disposable beverage containers entirely.

All, some, or none of the solutions mentioned may produce cleaner highways, but it is clear that the proposed solutions depend on the way in which problems and causes are defined. As in the example of flip-top cans, there are many rival explanations for why the American environment looks as it does, and these explanations can be categorized according to whether they deal with immediate, or proximate, causes (the can thrower), or societal conditions further removed from the actual pollution (priorities in using aluminum). Proximate causes are numerous and varied, but their inherent nature produces suggestions for moderate change involving relatively minor manipulation of the decision-making process. The societal type of explanation tends to spread the blame more widely and calls for more radical shifts in policy. Like interpreting the litter problem as an excess of containers and recommending recycling methods, a solution based on societal conditions is more difficult to achieve and less comprehensible to the average citizen.

The limited nature of immediate causes makes them more understandable. Like blaming the litter bug for litter, these questions seem to be more resolvable and may be considered first. The number of specific proximate explanations is large, but for purposes of analysis they can be divided into problems of information/communications, economics, and politics.

## PROXIMATE CAUSATION: INFORMATION/ COMMUNICATIONS

One factor that has inhibited the discussion of pollution problems for many years is the failure of policy makers to recognize that problems exist. Although individuals, including many politicians and bureaucrats, have become dissatisfied with the quality of their own environment, they have taken independent action to improve their immediate surroundings, often simply by transferring their household to a more desirable location. This private solution only complicates the societal solution, for new areas are opened up to the same human-behavior patterns that despoiled the older areas. Many policy makers remained blissfully uninformed about the pervasiveness and seriousness of the problem of environmental degradation, a situation chiefly evident to natural scientists.

These scientists—botanists, biologists, demographers, chemists and ecologists—discerned a heightened threat to public health by an increasingly degraded environment years ago. They failed to attract much attention until recently, however, when popularizers of scientific findings such as Barry Commoner and Rachel Carson raised the alarm with their books *Science and Survival* and *Silent Spring.*[1] In many instances the dangers have still not been demonstrated to everyone's satisfaction, as in the case of Reserve Mining, rival experts continuing to argue over the long-range effects of exposure to asbestos fibers on humans. For many years only a minority of scientists were willing to speak out against escalating pollution; this situation has only begun to change.

Some analysts believe the teaching of science embodies a built-in bias that prevents many of these dangers, such as the profligate overuse of insecticides, from being noticed by scientists themselves. Emerging scientists are trained to view their subject from an engineering perspective, as being composed of small "manageable" questions that can be answered before moving on to the next project. If scientists were themselves more involved in the theory of their discipline instead of in its application to solve problems as they arise, they might avoid many of the bad side effects of technology before they become problems of pollution.[2]

The increased separation of the natural sciences (the study of the natural world and the effects of people's uses of it) from the social sciences (the study of people and the demands they make on their social institutions, including government and the economy) contributed to past failure to take action against recognized dangers. Analysts such as Lynton K. Caldwell argued that had there been more communication between the different disciplines, many pollution problems might have been ameliorated earlier. Policy makers would have been alerted to the dangers of our increasingly complex technology and would have been encouraged to take action by an aroused and informed public opinion.[3] The obvious inference is that if people were informed about the nature of the effects of their wastes on their environment, they would alter their attitudes and behavior. This optimistic view is not entirely justified. It took from 1962, when Rachel Carson warned of the effects of DDT, to 1972, when EPA banned nearly all uses of DDT, for any official action to be taken.[4]

Policy makers at least need to be informed about how their policies affect the quality of air, water, and land before any reform action can realistically be expected. Even when policy makers understand the problem they must inform the public of the benefits to be derived from a cleaner environment in order to build support for action. Admittedly it takes more than education and scientific facts to persuade policy makers to act and for the public to urge them on to action. Many other factors intervene to prevent such a simple solution; however, it is necessary to begin somewhere, and there can be no beginning without information. Today's ecology movement is indebted to the early work of publicists who provided and continue to provide much-needed basic information.

## PROXIMATE CAUSATION: ECONOMICS

Another factor that has affected decisions about environmental matters is the method by which our society distributes goods held in common, a subject that many believe logically belongs in the realm of economics. Many ecologically aware economists and planners believe that pollution exists because its costs cannot be distributed properly by a free market economy, due to the public nature of certain natural resources. Their way of viewing pollution is best expressed by the concept "external diseconomies." Briefly, this theory means that pollution producers, who derive benefits from dumping wastes into the free sinks provided by their own (and everyone else's) natural resources, do not incorporate into their operating costs the expense of cleaning up those natural resources afterward. There is no reason for them to do so, given the present method of distributing goods in the marketplace. Air, land, and water have always been used as free sinks into which everyone throws whatever is of no utility to himself without regard for the condition in which the natural resource reaches the next user. Consequently, the whole community, not the individual waste dischargers, bears the cost of using natural resources as sinks.

Decision makers within all organizations using natural resources recognize the need to obtain clean raw materials for their own use and are willing to process the raw materials to produce the degree of purity needed for their own purposes. Many manufacturers, for example, must clean water at their intake pipes in order to prevent it from corroding their machinery. They are not willing to pay for cleaning the water they later dump into the same stream after they have used it. There is no incentive to do so, and no evident benefits, except the possible good will of downstream neighbors, accrue from such socially desirable behavior. According to economists, the treatment of residuals is irrational because the benefits derived from dirtying the natural resources belong to one set of policy makers and the cost of disposing of wastes is borne by a different group, often all of society. This does not preclude individuals involved in the first process from being included in the second group. The role of private citizens enjoying recreational facilities is quite different from that of making managerially rational decisions to degrade the environment, and the latter role dominates.

This type of argument is stated eloquently by the biologist Garrett Hardin, who has argued that the reason for the deterioration of our environment is the fact that natural resources are regarded by citizens as "free goods," available to all and the responsibility of none.[5] As in the case of all goods held in common by a community, there is a personal incentive to utilize the commonly held goods to and beyond their natural limits. While everyone can perceive the need to conserve commonly held goods such as water, land, and air, no one is personally motivated to do so unless all others act similarly. Each person is aware that the cumulative effect of everyone's dumping will eventually render the environment useless for any purpose other than a public trash heap. He is not motivated to cease using it for that purpose because even if he restrains himself there is nothing to prevent others from continuing their antisocial behavior, thus destroying the resource anyway.

This selfishness is exemplified by the behavior of lobster fishermen in an area in which the lobster population is being decimated by overharvesting. Each fisherman recognizes the need to utilize conservation methods in order for anyone to be able to catch lobsters in the future. Each harvester is nonetheless motivated by his immediate self-interest, and goes on putting down more and more lobster pots in the hope of increasing his personal share of the catch rather than making an individual sacrifice by reducing his efforts to snare a dying breed. As the catch becomes more scarce the need for conservation grows, along with the pressure for each fisherman to maximize his own share of the catch. This situation is analogous to that of air and water, for as they become dirtier and dirtier, it becomes evident that it would require a larger sacrifice in expenditures to turn the trend around. Each user, watching others dumping their untreated wastes into the surrounding environment, is further motivated to behave in a similar fashion himself, renouncing any effort to clean up.

The difficulty, as viewed from an economic point of view, is truly a problem of the distribution of resources. Everyone contributes some wastes to the environment. No one is motivated to reduce his contribution if he sees that others are not being induced to behave responsibly. The free market economy will not solve the problem because of its very nature. So long as open space, air, and water remain undervalued in their natural state, people and organizations will continue to dump their untreated wastes into these resources.

## PROXIMATE CAUSATION: POLITICAL-POWER DISTRIBUTION

Since under the present system there is no reason for individuals to clean up voluntarily, many policy makers have reluctantly concluded that the strong arm of government or some other coercive force must be exerted over everyone in order to force all to participate in the cleanup effort. This idea has existed for a number of years: Why, then, have efforts to remedy the situation proved less than adequate? Of the several explanations readily available, each represents another proximate or intervening cause of pollution. First among these is a political-power explanation. Every citizen of the United States is somewhat interested in seeing the environment improved. Every human user of water, air, and land has—or should have—reason to wish an improvement in the quality of these resources, at least in his immediate vicinity. The difficulty arises from the multiple roles everyone plays in society. More often than not, economic values prove more important to decision making than other, more peripheral social roles.

The president of the local rod and gun club, for example, may advocate open space for hunting and fishing on weekends. But during the week, in his role as chairman of the board of the community's major polluting industry, his viewpoint shifts dramatically. So long as he knows that he can escape to a local suburb or to a home in the country for his recreational needs on weekends, it may seem of little consequence to him that his industry pollutes the countryside nearest the factory and for some miles around. After all, he does not live there, and those who do, his lawyers argue, were aware of the plant's existence before they moved in. It is, therefore, their risk and responsibility.

Workers in the factory may share their employer's ambivalence. They, too, see the need for fresh air for their children to breathe, not only on weekends when the plant temporarily stops belching smoke, but also throughout the work week. Their overriding concern, however, is to provide those children with the necessities of life, and the only opportunity they perceive for earning a living may be the very factory that offends their sensibilities and harms their health, and they may even overlook the latter because of inadequate information about the degree of harm to health. This type of attitude is considerably strengthened by management's frequent reminders to them that government regulation may one day deprive them of all means of earning a livelihood. The claims of owners of economically marginal industries that they have been the victims of needless government regulation often increase worker's fears. While demands for better pollution controls may have forced some marginal operations out of business, environmentalism has proved to be a useful scapegoat for many management decisions that would have been made regardless of government regulation. The Hobson's choice (no choice at all) of either poor environment or unemployment so often offered to workers is exemplified by the pseudoboastful declaration commonly heard in towns particularly noted for obnoxious industrial odors that "That's the smell of money."

The ambivalence felt by many different role players is very real and often sincere, but the outcome more often than not is a decision that demonstrates less than maximum concern for environmental quality. The winners in most arguments, both within organizations and between them, have been those forces who favor continuing to use the environment for waste disposal. The kinds of representation that the two sides have when they confront each other in the political arena explain this situation. In court, for example, propollution forces are usually represented by legal counsel from large corporations, from trade associations representing industrial interests, or from municipal governments. To the opposing side often rally volunteer lawyers, frequently idealistic recent graduates from law school.

These lawyers are not necessarily incompetent, but they are often pitted against the superior numbers and quality of human resources mustered by the propollution forces. Public pollution hearings are filled with scientific information from experts in the running of sewage-treatment plants, city dumps, and incinerators, as well as from engineers employed by industry. All are expert in emphasizing the exorbitant cost of cleaning up a minute amount of dirt and in minimizing the significance of that dirt. Some scientists regularly testify before judges and congressmen concerning the need for more unpolluted land, air, and water, but many of these people are unpaid or underpaid; their organizations are entirely dependent on voluntary public subscriptions—not a limitless source of funds. Often such public interest groups have had their tax-exempt status removed or face its imminent removal because of their clear advocacy role in such disputes. They must register as political lobbyists, which indeed they are, if one defines that term as an advocate for one side in a public controversy. The generous salaries of corporation counsels, on the other hand, are deducted as part of the normal expense of doing business for an industry. Ironically, management does not consider the cost of cleaning wastes a normal expense, and this is one reason why such companies as Reserve Mining can afford to spend more on legal fees defending present practices than in developing new methods for waste disposal.

As happens so often with other types of government regulation, agencies frequently become co-opted by the very interests they were created to control, so that persons concerned with the technology, financing, and other facilitative problems involved in pollution control will come to share more common interests with each other than with antipollution forces. The latter, often without permanent, well paid technical experts, are put into the position of demanding results without being able to recommend specific methods for achieving greater policy impact. The division of power is clearly in favor of polluters.[6]

## PROXIMATE CAUSATION: LACK OF ADMINISTRATIVE COORDINATION

Inequity in the distribution of clout in the American political system is not the only political explanation available. The conflict model of decision making is not the only political model. Some analysts prefer to attribute the lack of impact of our official pollution-control policy to a lack of coordination rather than to a maldistribution of influence. These people view our inability to achieve a cleaner environment as a result of administrative inefficiency, not as a result of an imbalance in the relative distribution of political power.

A variety of policy makers at all levels and in all branches of government are continually making decisions that affect the environment. Such decisions frequently contradict one another and often act at cross purposes. The decisions of different governmental agencies may often lead to contradictory policies without conscious rivalry or disagreement between the officials involved. For example, local government could obtain considerable savings if metropolitan and suburban areas were to band together to develop large-scale sewage-treatment facilities, incinerators, and sanitary landfills. Instead, numerous units on the local level compete for space and funds from taxpayers and the federal government. Jealous of their own autonomy and fearful of being outvoted and overcharged by a consortium, many mayors, city managers, and planners cling to their own decision-making authority and refuse to enter into any cooperative venture.

The traditional rivalries among coequal administrations are echoed in the interrelationship of agencies created to deal with different problems. With a plethora of special administrative units whose sole responsibility consists of functions such as water resources, water-pollution control, highway construction, zoning restrictions, air-pollution control, and solid-waste disposal, there is little cooperation vertically within the same region. Often decisions made by one agency (to burn off dumps, for example) come into direct conflict with a policy developed by others in the air-pollution-control district. Sometimes the short-run gains made by one decision maker are more than offset by the long-term difficulties he has created for others. It is often true that the original decision maker does not have to face the new problems, but they might have been avoided altogether if some early cooperative efforts to engage in trade-offs had been made. Given the fragmented nature of local and state governments as they exist in this country today, lack of coordination and cooperation sometimes adds to environmental problems that might otherwise have been ameliorated. This is comparable to what economists describe as external diseconomies. Separate sets of decision makers formulating pieces of policy independently of each other often contribute to each other's problems.

Without the motivation of a common outlook or the ability to view the problem of environmental control as a whole, ad hoc decisions are commonplace. This problem is two-pronged. The first aspect is more obvious: Decision makers concerned with a narrow function or a small geographical area tend to view their task myopically and may opt for a solution that causes more problems for their nearest neighbors than it solves for themselves. Cooperative decisions would be more satisfactory. The second aspect is the problem of long-term and short-term gains. Frequently government's decisions are the least costly only in the short run. The limited tenure of office holders at all levels of government makes these decisions most expedient, but when problems are merely postponed into the not-so-distant future, the community ends by paying more to solve the same problem serially than it would have if a radical solution had originally been chosen. For example, the decision to break ground for a new sewage-treatment plant is a difficult one for any city administration to make but in the long run is a more economical move for the municipality than updating an inadequate plant and meeting emergency situations with ever-increasing frequency.

Problems of coordination do not exclusively exist on the local level. They are equally prevalent on the state and federal levels and between the three levels of government. States that could develop large-scale endeavors and produce a more equitable and efficient operation face the intrusion of rivalries of sovereignty and competition in attracting businesses and industries. In the federal bureaucracy, an even larger and more incomprehensible behemoth, these problems become magnified. Examples are rife of policies adopted in one part of the bureaucracy that directly contradict those in others. For years the Interstate Commerce Commission has encouraged the increasing depletion of our raw materials by giving a more favorable rate for transportation of virgin materials than for scrap that could be utilized for the same purposes.[7] At the same time, EPA is actively engaged in a campaign to influence governmental agencies themselves to utilize recycled materials whenever possible, yet governmental policies make the relative costs of these materials noncompetitive.

The lack of cooperative effort among federal agencies is frequently due not so much to ignorance of each other's goals but to opposition to them.The attitudes adopted by agency officials themselves reflect competitive interests that the various agencies of government represent. Thus, the Department of Agriculture remains the greatest contender for continued use of pesticides and herbicides to increase farm production, while EPA and CEQ argue against them. The Federal Energy Administration, created in 1974 to deal with the fuel shortage, has concentrated much of its attention on challenging the need for national air-quality standards established earlier by EPA. Today many of the arguments between industry and environmentalists are mirrored in the rivalry between these two federal agencies.

Municipal officials rail at Washington for not providing sufficient funds to assure the success of their municipal sewage-treatment programs. In its turn, EPA threatens and postures against municipal authorities for not meeting implementation-plan deadlines for cleaning up their sewage. There are problems of coordination on all levels and among all levels of government. Some of these stem from a lack of planning and the incapacity of human beings to incorporate all factors into their decision making.[8] Others, more difficult of solution, are the result of differences among policy makers of values and opinions about priorities for American society.

## PRIMARY CAUSATION: POPULATION SIZE

Discussion of immediate causes of specific pollution problems presents the difficulty of resolving environmental problems without facing larger issues. Indeed, most people's attitudes toward the smaller political and economic questions stem from their orientation on the much larger, philosophical problems of the quality of life in this country. Generally these philosophical questions revolve around two issues: the optimal number of people our society can support and the quality of life toward which our national goals should be directed.

The simple fact that there are more people in the United States producing, using, and discarding trash and unassimilable junk accounts for their abundance. People are a part of pollution by definition, for they have altered the environment ever since their arrival on this planet. For a long time the population was sufficiently small and widely distributed enough to allow natural forces to clean up human wastes before they became health hazards for their own creators. Once the population reached a certain density the dispersal of concentrated wastes into the larger environment beyond human habitation became necessary.

We have reached this threshold of population size in the United States and in most locations around the world. We can no longer afford to simply throw our litter farther away into the water, land, and air around us, because it, or that of our neighbors, returns to pollute our surroundings. Regardless of whether it is our own litter or someone else's, these solid, liquid, and gaseous wastes are too copious for us to ignore or for the natural reactions in the earth, air, and water to assimilate. On the simplest level, the explanation for increased pollution problems is the fact that more and more people are occupying the same limited space on a finite globe. The methods of waste disposal that worked efficiently in the past will no longer suffice. We need alternative solutions to the problems of Spaceship Earth.

Increases in the production of wastes may well be outstripping any control efforts because of the nature of population growth. Between 1830 and 1930 the world's population doubled from 1 to 2 billion. In only thirty years, by 1960, it had reached 3 billion, and in fifteen years, by 1975, a world population of 4 billion existed. Demographers anticipate that by the year 2000 the total world population will reach the level of 6.5 billion. This growth pattern is reflected in our own country. In 1915 the U.S. population was a modest 100 million; by 1970 it had more than doubled to over 200 million, a level that is already too high for some people's taste. After the 1970 census it was estimated that in the years remaining in the twentieth century the U.S. population would easily reach the 250-million mark. Reduction in the U.S. birth rate during the first half of the 1970s has cast uncertainty upon the accuracy of future projections. For the first time in U.S. history the fertility rate fell below the replacement level of 2.1 children per couple. Because of the disproportionate number of people presently in their reproductive years, however, it may be 2040 A.D. before the total U.S. population levels off, even assuming no increase in fertility rates from the present all-time low.[9]

## PRIMARY CAUSATION: TECHNOLOGY

If population is growing exponentially, the second cause of pollution, industrialization, is growing even faster. "Modern living through chemistry" and other types of new technology have indeed changed the standard of living in this country. But also increased is the hazard that each of us faces from such formerly unrecognized problems as radiation poisoning and the gradual buildup of chemical poisons in the food chain from insecticides, herbicides, and artificial fertilizers. Many scientists argue convincingly that since natural organic wastes produced by people and other animals are much less dangerous and objectionable than are the by-products of modern civilization, industrialized nations have a near monopoly on environmental degradation. The United States, with only about 5.5 percent of the world's population, consumes anywhere from 20 percent to over 40 percent of the planet's most valuable raw materials. The notion that pollution is a problem of affluence rather than of sheer numbers has some basis. Industrial by-products account for the majority of both organic and artificial wastes dumped into our waterways each year. Factory smokestacks, together with the internal-combustion engine, have produced a metropolitan air-pollution level unattainable by such natural causes as forest fires. Unforeseen by-products of our constantly evolving technology create major hazards that the average citizen is incapable of assessing for himself. The public finds itself confronting mysterious and formerly unheard-of dangers with increasing frequency. These threats range from immediate effects to individuals, such as the effects from inhaling or drinking asbestos fibers, to long-range eco-system inpacts such as the destruction of the ozone belt of the earth's atmosphere by gases released from aerosol cans. Few citizens are capable of evaluating the seriousness of such phenomena, a situation that only reemphasizes the natural scientist's role in determining how policy makers must respond to demands.[10]

The field of energy consumption illustrates the escalating problem of technological pollution. As our society has become more industrialized, energy consumption has become one of our greatest pollution producers, although it is an industry that we consider vital to our continued well-being. The agricultural sector of the economy is as dependent as any other on the energy supply. The farmer who formerly rode horses for transportation and recreation and plowed his fields with the same animals today may own numerous pieces of powered farm equipment, two cars for transportation, possibly a boat or snowmobile for recreation, or even an airplane for business and/or pleasure. This individual accounts for an energy and raw materials consumption equal to that of many of his predecessors. His siblings, who have moved off the farm to the city, consume more material things and contribute even more pollution through their highly mechanized mode of life. Even if they were no more numerous than their earlier counterparts today's Americans would nevertheless be contributing more heavily to environmental damage simply because of the technological age in which they live.

One solution to the previously mentioned problem of voluntary population restriction may in fact be helping to complicate and escalate the problem of technological pollution. The desire to increase the standard of living of the whole family has motivated a decrease in the number of offspring. Among American families in the nineteenth century it was not uncommon to have six or eight children in one generation. In the mid-1970s one to three offspring is the norm. A typical U.S. family no longer utilizes most of its limited income to purchase food, clothing, and housing for eight or ten members, but a family of four today has innumerable options for disposing of its "superfluous" income, including multiple cars, color television sets, and a home away from home in the form of a camper, vacation home, or boat. The production and consumption of material goods has not gone down, despite conscious decisions on the part of the parent generation to limit its progeny. The damage to the environment goes unchecked; in fact it increases drastically.

In the past many wastes produced by large families were primarily organic and assimilable by nature. Today, with their increased affluence, families are capable of making demands on the economy for such sophisticated gadgets as snowmobiles. These new mechanical marvels cause pollution not only during their production, but throughout their period of use. They make continuing demands on the total energy supply and pollute the landscape with noise, fumes, and finally with the hulk of yet another no-longer-valued mechanical device. Reduction in family size does not by itself engender environmental peace but may contribute to increasing pollution—at least in a rich, industrialized nation.

Every technological innovation does not necessarily produce filthy air, land, and water. Our advanced technology may be directed toward cleaning up the environment rather than further degrading it. Sewage-treatment plants and centers for converting solid wastes into new energy sources are two ways by which technology can respond to increasing pollution. The most widespread dangers of disease exist in the least industrialized areas of the world because of lack of adequate sanitation. The original hazard identified by pollution controllers—waterborne and airborne disease—is still most prevalent in the least industrialized parts of the world. When sewage runs in the streets it is hardly realistic to maintain that pollution is not a problem because of low mercury contamination. Many developing nations think to solve their problems by the application of the very technology that has become the major problem for advanced nations.

The consumption of material goods, whose manufacture contributes so heavily to environmental damage, increases each year more rapidly than does population. Technology has increased pollution and has drastically changed its nature. Many technological hazards remain without solutions. Atomic generators continue to build up radioactive wastes while their advocates reassure the public that future scientists will discover fail-safe methods of disposal. Workers in the asbestos industry are encouraged to remain at their jobs while medical experts argue about the likelihood of their contracting cancer. Increased technological proficiency is a two-edged sword: Without it, the increase in population will go unchecked and increased demands for food, energy, and other necessities of life will not be met; with it, the quality of life bequeathed to the surviving population will become less and less valuable.

## PRIMARY CAUSATION: GROWTHMANSHIP

Although there are differences of opinion about the relative importance of population and industrialization, most persons concerned about the present state of the environment agree that both contribute to pollution. The importance assigned to each is a function of how far advanced technologically (or how far gone, depending on one's point of view) the particular part of the world is where one resides. Regardless of whether we consider population or industrialization the more guilty, there exists a third problem, which precedes and perhaps gives rise to both: the philosophy of a society toward growth. Having become accustomed to the idea of a constantly expanding economy, most Americans anticipate that the material goods available to them will increase each year. We have traditionally measured our standard of living by per capita income as well as by per capita Gross National Product produced by our economy.The argument that we must continue to expand our Gross National Product each year in order to achieve further "progress" has found its proponents in most of our present government decision makers, who are firmly committed to this type of policy. From a political point of view, this state of affairs would seen inevitable.

The simplest method for achieving the goal of constantly expanding economic capacity, according to this philosophy, is to increase the population, thereby creating an ever-expanding source of labor and more importantly an expanding market for additional goods and services. Many economists argue against a stable population base on just such grounds.[11] Of course it will be necessary for the economy to increase its production of food, clothing, shelter, and energy if each new individual is to consume at the same rate as did his predecessors. Every worker in the economy, from educators to used-car salesmen, recognizes the threat to his own job security if his clientele decreases. It takes no urging to jump from need for employment to need for a market, and most simply interpreted, that market takes the form of more people.

The goal of rising expectations, or, as expressed in American society, social mobility, contributes to the commitment to growth in our economy. This is the process by which the have-nots observe the material possessions of the haves and demand that their own consumption patterns be raised to that level. Paradoxically, even if the population were eventually to level off, larger amounts of commodities would have to be produced in order to provide an ever-rising standard of living for the fixed numbers of residents.[12]

Despite the several strategies open for improving the lot of the poorest members in our society, including a more even redistribution of the available wealth among the population; nevertheless, the only solution to the problem of rising demands seriously contemplated by most policy makers in our nation is to increase the total pie to be distributed. Thus, the government seems committed to the idea that in order for wealth to "trickle down" to the masses the entire economy must grow and prosper. Those persons and groups who occupy the lowest niches in the economy have been conditioned to share this belief. Economists committed to an ever-expanding economy argue that efforts to reduce man's alteration of his environment will only postpone the gains still to be made by the poorest segments of our population. This is true whether the contrast is between nations or between the rich and poor of one nation. The less industrialized nations regard the effort to develop a global environmental-control policy as a move to freeze developing nations at their present state of disadvantage and to make permanent the present disequilibrium that exists in terms of the percentages of raw materials consumed by each country.

An ever-expanding economy, while remaining one of the most obvious reasons for our deteriorating environment, is also a forceful argument against many kinds of pollution control. In its purest form advocacy of economic growth leads to encouraging a constantly expanding population and an increasing GNP. Thus the philosophy of growthmanship exists for both productivity and population. If the only way to maintain a rising standard of living is to continue to grow and if pollution is attributable to both technology and population, then clearly the attitude toward growth in this country is a contributing factor to pollution. Growthmanship may be looked upon as *the* primary cause since both population and productive capacity continue to expand because of our commitment to this policy.[13]

So long as we remain committed to the idea that the only way to improve the lot of the poorest in our society is to improve the lot of all, including the richest, our primary public policy goal will be a constantly expanding economy. Those who are worst off would still have the most to lose in an ecologically sound society, a "fact" about which business and governmental leaders are eager to inform the poor. The poorest segment of the population will remain at the same level relative to the rest of the population; the only thing that may change will be their absolute level of poverty, since as the standard of living for all improves, it will rise for them too. If we are content to measure our success and happiness in terms of material possessions, the economy will continue to expand unendingly. A generation that continues to believe that it must have things better than its preceding generation will of necessity demand bigger houses, more cars, more labor-saving devices, and other material goods. Since the production of all these things pollutes the environment, as the standard of living continues to rise so will the level of pollution. So long as we remain committed to the philosophy that more means better there is little chance for reducing man's impact on his environment.

## SUMMARY

The combination of three factors gives us a reasonable explanation for the existence of pollution. First, for many years our expanding population has dumped its wastes into a limited environment whose assimilative capacity has now been reached. Consequently, the dirt created over the years is becoming more evident to those concerned enough to observe it. Second, technology has proceeded more than apace with population. The more affluent our society has become, the more goods and services it has produced, together with their natural by-product—more pollution. Third and last, people's attitudes, including their devotion to the ever-expanding economy, have created within the whole population the expectation that its standard of living will rise as measured in terms of material possessions. In order to achieve that goal, it has become necessary to increase the per capital production and consumption of goods each year.

Numerous explanations of why the United States today faces significant problems of environmental deterioration range from all-inclusive, basic causes, such as increased population and the technology of the twentieth century, to basic tenets of our philosophy and culture that cause modern Americans to approve of life in a throwaway economy. Other explanations of why our efforts to clean up have met with less than complete success range from problems of perception, to economic arguments over the distribution of the costs of disposing of wastes, to political factors outlining the relative power of interests in society and efficiency in administration. Although the different theories of causation have not been evaluated, it is important to keep them in mind when considering the various suggestions for solutions to our problems in the following chapters.

Most readers of the preceding pages will have already reached some tentative conclusions about the relative importance of each of the suggested causes. Environmental problems and our failure to cope adequately with them are probably due to a combination of these factors. They do not act independently of each other, but a solution to one would probably not eliminate the total problem either. Any program designed to deal with the environment or correct the mistakes of the past will have to take into consideration a combination of the causes outlined in this chapter.

## NOTES

1. Rachel Carson, *Silent Spring* (Cambridge, Mass.: Houghton Mifflin, 1962); Barry Commoner, *Science and Survival* (New York: Viking Press, 1962).

2. Barry Commoner, op. cit.

3. Lynton K. Caldwell, *Environmental Studies* (Bloomington, Ind.: Institute of Public Administration, 1967).

4. Council on Environmental Quality, *Fourth Annual Report*, p. 125.

5. Garrett Hardin, "Tragedy of the Commons," *Science*, 162 (December 13, 1968): 1243–48.

6. Prominent among advocates of the political-power explanation of pollution are such groups as Nader's Raiders, who have documented the political ties of major governmental decision makers and polluters. See, for example, David Zwick and Marcy Benstock, *Water Wasteland* (New York: Grossman, 1971).

7. SCRAP v. United States, 353 Federal Supplement 317 (D.D.C. 1972).

8. Public-administration specialists are prime promoters of this explanation of lack of integrated pollution control. See, for example, Lynton K. Caldwell, *Environment* (Garden City, N.Y.: Anchor Books, 1971).

9. Council on Environmental Quality, *Fifth Annual Report*, 1974, p. 251. Prominent among thinkers who believe that the population is a primary cause of pollution are Paul R. and Anne H. Ehrlich, *Population, Resources, Environment* (San Francisco: W.H. Freeman, 1970).

10. For a discussion of various technological problems, see Barry Commoner, op. cit.; Maurice F. Strong, ed., *Who Speaks for Earth?* (New York: W.W. Norton, 1973); Huey D. Johnson, *No Deposit—No Return* (Reading, Mass.: Addison-Wesley, 1970).

11. For a popular exposition of this point of view, see Rudolf Klein, "The Trouble With a Zero Growth World," *The New York Times Magazine*, Sunday, June 2, 1974, pp. 14–84.

12. For a comparison between the arguments of those proponents of reduced growth and those of continued expansion, see Donella H. Meadows, et al., *The Limits to Growth* (New York: Universe Books, 1972); and H.D.S. Cole, et al., *Models of Doom* (New York: Universe Books, 1973).

13. For a review of the literature concerning the arguments about growth, see Hazel Henderson, "Ecologists Versus Economists," *Harvard Business Review* (July–August, 1973): 1–10.

CHAPTER SEVEN

# Solutions to Pollution: The Little Questions

Pollution is a complex phenomenon created by multiple causes for which there are no simple solutions. This does not preclude proponents of suggested remedies. The more time policy makers spend considering pollution and the more interests become involved in the discussion, the more numerous recommendations become. These recommendations parallel the kinds of causes already suggested and lend themselves to the same kinds of categories into which the problems have been divided: modest, specific, directed programs and general, large-scale, wholistic solutions. It is with the modest programs that this chapter deals: Like the problems that give rise to them, they are the easier to understand.

Frequently, proponents of new solutions are motivated by dissatisfaction with the impact of present programs. They thereby demonstrate their implicit belief that they can accurately predict the outcome of their own policy proposals, an assumption that may or may not be valid. In discussing proposed new methods for handling environmental matters it is therefore useful to analyze not only the intended goals of such methods but also the likelihood of achievement of those goals.

## THE FREE-ENTERPRISE MODEL

Most economic solutions to pollution stem from the idea that the real cause of pollution is society's treatment of natural resources as free, public goods of no particular worth and no specific ownership, which may be claimed on a "first come, first served" basis. This commonality of approach can yet divide into a variety of solutions, depending on whether one goes by the laissez-faire model of economics or by the newer welfare economics. The most traditional economic solution is expressed by the belief that the best things in life should not be free and should be priced in proportion to their utility to the consumer. According to this school of thought, environmental degradation results precisely because users of earth, air, and water are not fully charged for the benefits they derive from these resources. The logical solution to pollution is to allow the price of these basic commodities to float free until the "invisible hand" of the marketplace determines a fair price for them based on what people are willing to pay, which is in turn based on supply and demand.

This process will ultimately determine the uses to which such resources will be put. In many locations at the present time, clean water is sold to various users at different rates. The small-scale domestic user is charged disproportionately more than the large-scale industrial user, a fact that encourages the latter's use of processes that waste water because of his lack of incentive to conserve the available supply. To correct this the pure free-enterprise model would charge everyone at the same rate. More importantly, the rate would be uncontrolled and would rise as demand increased, until the supply became so restricted that the cost would be prohibitive except to those who used water for the most profitable enterprises. Pursuing this argument to its logical conclusion, if those who favor utilizing natural resources as sinks can outbid those who would prefer a cleaner environment for recreational and other purposes, they should be allowed to do so.

To take one example, that of offshore drilling, the government auctions leases for oil and mineral rights in the continental shelf. If those interests in society such as shell fishermen and beach owners, who view the oil industry as a threat to their livelihood, can outbid it for the oil rights and then decide to sit on these rights rather than exploit them, that is up to the interests involved. The distribution of resources in our society is such that the outcome of such competitive bidding is, however, a foregone conclusion. There is no inequity in this, because if oil corporations possess the needed investment capital, that fact alone demonstrates that society benefits so much from their activities that it has made oil production sufficiently profitable to allow oil corporations to outbid competitors for the same resources. This type of policy would consider all natural resources auctionable to the highest bidder and would place sports fishermen in the position of attempting to outbid all the chemical and stock-butchering industries along the Mississippi River for the assimilative capacity of that river. The managers of the Mississippi River would of course realize a greater profit in utilizing it as a sink than as a recreation area.

Proponents of the auction of natural resources are willing to accept these kinds of outcomes because it is their contention that relatively clean air and water and unspoiled areas are valued differentially by various individuals in society. Those who value them and need them should be willing to pay for them, since public funds should not be used for goods and services for a privileged minority seeking to impose its values on others. Poverty-stricken families have more important priorities than recreation; they must attend to employment and cheaper commodities. These people, it is argued, are being denied necessities while public funds are used to buy up wilderness areas for the enjoyment of the backpacking set, who wield influence with Congress. It is not reasonable to assume that no clean air and water or recreation space will eventually be left because of industrial expansion. As clean air, water, and land become more scarce, those who value them more highly will be willing to pay more for them. Asthma sufferers who require cleaner air would be willing to exchange some of their other commodities and services for a better environment, whereas those with better health would not feel this need so intensely.[1]

Is it possible to make some predictions about the eventual outcome of letting fresh air, clean water, and uncluttered land seek their own price levels? A minority may be willing to make some sacrifices for such natural resources, either because of a greater need or because of personal values, but ability does not always accompany willingness. The number of asthmatic children a steel worker in Gary, Indiana has will not be neatly correlated with his ability to buy a summer retreat in the upper peninsula of Michigan. While it is true that the poor need to eat before they can use elaborate recreation facilities, it is also true that they must breathe before they can eat. If we reach the point where only the most affluent can afford to own living quarters in an unpolluted area, we will have confirmed the belief of many in our society that only a minority wants to pay for a clean environment. This belief does not take into account the inequities in income and available resources throughout our society and eventually condemns those without large resources to no clean air, earth, or water at all. Certain segments of all societies have always been able to afford unpolluted environments. Some have even been able to improve on them, as George S. Kaufman's comments about Moss Hart's estate in Bucks County, Pennsylvania indicate: "This is what God could have done if He'd had money."[2] The real question for environmental-policy makers and for experts in other areas is: How widely are such amenities as clean air and water to be distributed in our society?

## PLANNING THROUGH COST/ BENEFIT ANALYSIS

Most policy makers and reformers seem willing to accept the notion that the uses to which we put our land, water, and air need to be decided in a less than totally free market situation. But present methods of handling pollution control are considered to be uneconomical for society because they result in inefficient allocations of societal resources for pollution control. Contributors to pollution who could most economically clean up are not expected to do any more than those whose wastes are extraordinarily expensive to treat. A more efficient management of resources would procure more pollution control at the same cost to society. For example, it is undesirable to demand that all factories producing the same type of product reduce their wastes by the same percentage. Some factories are clearly better able to reduce their wastes, being newer or having had some cleaner kinds of manufacturing processes originally installed. Others occupy positions in relatively unused parts of the environment and distribute their wastes into a less polluted area where the assimilative capacity of the environment is greater. It would be more economical for society, so the argument goes, to utilize the available natural sinks to their maximum capacity as repositories for those wastes most difficult to treat and to require only those dischargers with the cheapest wastes to clean them up.

Making such kinds of discriminatory decisions within the present regulatory framework is obviously impractical because of the inequities and burdens that they would place upon some types of polluters. The solution to this dilemma is to turn over to the same set of planners all decisions having to do with residuals management in a given area. A single group of technical experts will be able to evaluate the costs and benefits to be derived from treating wastes and determine what level of purity any specific area can afford. The utility of water, air, and soil for disposing of wastes has a quantifiable value easily expressed in dollars and cents, the cost of treating those wastes. Reduction of wastes also creates calculable benefits for distribution to all or a portion of the population in the area by way of better or increased recreation facilities, reduction in the cost of treating water for consumption, and reduction in health and property losses due to pollution.

Such economic calculations are based on the concept of marginal utility. The additional benefits derived from greater purity of water and air and from additional areas set aside for recreation will level off once a certain quality of environment is achieved. Conversely, the costs of further waste reduction will rise steeply after the application of primary and secondary techniques, since the technology for advanced treatment is progressively expensive. An optimal solution to every pollution problem exists; it only remains for policy makers to find the solution through the incorporation of all relevant values into their model.[3]

The cost/benefit strategy has considerable appeal for many persons who are dissatisfied with existing environmental policy, especially conservationists. Certainly this is an understandable position for ecologists to assume. They, more than others, recognize the interdependency of all living things and see the futility in continuing to assign environmental problems to discrete political units that compete rather than cooperate in making decisions. There is no arguing with the fact that multiple use of the same resource eliminates the motivation of any particular waste discharger to clean up.

The question remains: What are the likely outcomes of using cost/benefit analysis to prescribe the uses to which our available land, water and air in any region are to be put? Before this question, another must first be answered: Who is likely to make these decisions? According to economists and planners, the answer is: themselves. The literature is replete with theoretical models showing how the optimal quality of land, air, or water for a given area can be derived from estimates of the benefits and costs for various types and degrees of residuals reduction.

Free enterprise economists argue that different persons in society place different values on a clean environment. Many environmentalists would also credit themselves with the ability to estimate the benefits and costs to be derived from any system of treatment, but their calculations do not often resemble those projected by economists and planners. The most convinced model builders do not believe that any one person can assign objective values to all the parameters to be considered in any single river basin or airshed—an explanation for the existence of experts in a multitude of fields. The presence of experts still does not determine which one will be asked to make the evaluation of any given cost or benefit. To whom, for example, would a systems analyst turn for a price to attach to the damage done to one Gary, Indiana child's lungs by inhaling $x$ pounds of lead each year; a pediatrician practicing in Gary or one whose clients live in Beverly Hills? Should he ask an M.D. in the Public Health Service who saw no reason to restrict the experimental distribution of thalidomide a few years ago? An expert in the effects of air pollutants employed by U.S. Steel, or one employed by the Environmental Defense Fund?

While any set of environmental planners seems capable of quantifying the costs and benefits for a specific environmental-control program, another set of technocrats will challenge the first group's assumptions.[4] When it comes time for policy makers to select an approach, much will depend on the advice they have been given. Laymen responsible for directing public policy will seek expert advice in such technical matters as pollution control, but experts differ among themselves, and the really crucial decision is the selection of experts who make the necessary evaluations of costs and benefits.

If we disregard the question of who *should* be making these evaluations and consider only what is likely to happen, the most logical decision is to choose persons with experience in the area, in other words, the very bureaucrats whose "ineffectual" methods are to be replaced by rational planning. The United States has had a program of environmental control for many years. It has indeed worked, to the satisfaction of the dischargers if not to the satisfaction of environmentalists. The latter expect a more favorable outcome if a different method of reaching decisions is used, but interest groups who are dissatisfied with environmental-quality achievements in the past should consider whether the same administrators who sought to utilize the total assimiliative capacity of the environment in the past are likely to produce substantially different results when asked to evaluate benefits and costs under the new system.

## THE USER-CHARGE MODEL

A third method of regulating the environment proposed by some economists who criticize the present system represents a compromise between the free-enterprise method and the totally planned cost/benefit method discussed in the first two sections of this chapter. Utilizing parts of both methods, the emergent suggestion is that policy goals (the condition of the environment) be set politically but that as many operational decisions as possible be left to the economic marketplace. This method has been labeled variously as the effluent-charge or emissions-tax system.

The underlying idea is to allow the individual waste discharger considerable discretion in the method he chooses to deal with his own wastes. The assumption behind this method is that if residuals managers are given free rein to deal with problems they will devise more economically efficient solutions for the whole society. This is preferred over tying all dischargers to the same type of treatment or requiring them to reduce their wasteload by a specified percentage. It has been noted, quite legitimately, that creating more numerous and more complex added-on or end-of-process techniques may not be the most economical solution to wastes, even though it is currently favored by present administrative and tax laws. If the individual user were allowed to choose his own method, including changes in manufacturing techniques, he might very well discover relatively less expensive methods of achieving the same result.

Rather than insisting on an equal degree of treatment for all wastes, the effluent-charge method allows wastes that prove resistant to treatment to use the maximum assimilative capacity of the environment. Dischargers will thus treat easily reduced wastes more thoroughly to avoid payment of large user fees and society's available resources for pollution control will be more efficiently utilized to tackle problems that are most capable of being ameliorated. Once initial effluent charges have been set for strength and volume of each type of discharge, it is presumed that the system will become nearly self-regulating. Effluent dischargers will be motivated to keep their wastes within the limits of a certain volume and strength of waste. The governmental or quasi-public authority established to administer the program will use the fees collected for treating the remaining wastes so that the receiving air, water, and land will not become degraded below the level set for them.[5]

Before we accept the notion that one advantage to the fee system over present methods of regulation is that it will be fairly automatic and will not require large administrative expenditures to keep it in operation, it is important to inquire into exactly how the method is expected to function. Will this method indeed be as automatic in administration as claimed? Once the individual waste discharger has been informed of the costs for discharging a given kind of waste, can he be trusted to inform the authorities of the amount and volume of waste he indeed discharges each day? If the behavior of waste dischargers under the permit system is an indicator of their propensity to evade controls, he cannot. Monitoring devices placed at discharge points must be kept in constant operation to obtain any accurate record of the amounts of waste actually discharged. One of the greatest weaknesses of the present permit system is the limited number of checks taken at outflow pipes. It is possible for waste dischargers to avoid detection by judicious selection of times to release large slugs of wastes: on particularly windy days, when stream flow is high, or at 2:00 A.M., when few enraged citizens and fewer pollution-control officials are present to notice the sudden stench.

If equally infrequent checks determine the fees an individual user must pay under the effluent-charge system, there will be just as much potential for slippage in administering these charges as there now exists in convincing users to adhere to the conditions of their permits. Under the user-charge system there would be no built-in opportunity for users to apply for special variances and postponements of enforcement; however, numerous possibilities for negotiation will arise concerning such subjects as the proper measurement of waste loads and the calculations of complex fees based on multiple kinds of wastes. Industries and municipalities with their resident experts in pollution control will, no doubt, resist accepting the administrative agencies' decisions on these subjects, just as they now object to agency regulations under the permit system.

One difficulty with the permit system is responsiveness to change. As more population and industry build up in an area, the environment becomes gradually more degraded with the granting on an ad hoc basis of increasing numbers of permits to dump. Sufficient attention is seldom given to the cumulative effect each permit has on the total environment. The question is: What would be the effect of increases in industrial output and population on the effluent-charge system? Let us imagine that a given fee has been determined for each unit of a given substance—for example, carbon dioxide—discharged. What happens when the population grows and additional cars are added to the highways? The owners of the new cars will be affected by the same kinds of economic constraints as the owners of older cars and will therefore seek to pay the user tax at approximately the same level. Consequently, increased carbon-dioxide dispersal in the atmosphere will increase carbon-dioxide concentration unless or until the charge is increased per unit of carbon dioxide. The appropriate charge to levy on each kind of pollutant will have to be frequently reassessed in a society with increasing population, affluence, and industrial capacity. The environment will become progressively more polluted without this frequent reassessment of fees as more and more individuals, industries, and municipalities choose to pay discharge fees.

The fees collected for some wastes, especially organic wastes dumped into waterways, would be most efficiently used for communal treatment facilities. Gradually increasing revenues would be utilized to treat increasing waste loads, presumably to the same degree that old waste loads were treated. If the facility in question is not upgraded this can only result in an increased absolute burden on the environment: Removing eighty percent of the biochemical oxygen demand (BOD) from the organic wastes of 200 people results in more BOD being discharged into the water than removing eighty percent of BOD for 100 people. The only way to maintain the same level of environmental quality in the face of increased population is to increase the rate that each individual user pays. The present permit system does necessitate a new administrative procedure each time an additional unit enters the system and ought to also require a new decision each time the load on presently existing treatment plants is increased. Effluent charges must also be revised as additional or increased factors enter the picture, if the same quality of environment is to be maintained.

Effluent charges are one method by which administrators could seek to implement the decision to maintain a given quality of the environment. Far from being a self-regulating or automatic method by which policy decisions can be permanently made, it will provoke cries of injustice each time waste dischargers see the ground rules shift under them and effluent fees changed, like permits, to conform to new conditions. Increasing waste production will unavoidably result either in greater efforts to cleanse the environment or in a more degraded environment. The same political and economic factors that affect the present permit system will influence decisions made within the framework of an effluent-charge system. Whether or not cost-benefit analysis or the user-charge model for decisions will result in any different outcomes for public policy is a matter for speculation.

## POLITICAL SOLUTIONS: LEVEL OF ADMINISTRATION

Supplementing and paralleling some of the economic solutions are several suggestions for changes in political and administrative frameworks. First among these, a strategy suggested by many proponents of more stringent controls, is the suggestion that the authority for enforcement be transferred from the local to the state, and from the state to the federal level of government. There, it is assumed, local economic interests will be less influential in the process of enforcement. Certainly such a strategy has good theoretical grounds on which to stand; it is rational for those who view themselves as losing on one level to attempt to "escalate the conflict," to increase the size of the decision-making body in order to alter the outcomes. This tactic has been used in the past; the history of pollution control has consisted of a gradual increase of federal responsibility. Following the shift to a greater federal enforcement power has been evidence of considerable increase in abatement efforts in this country.

The question of causation remains: Have policy alterations really resulted from the change in location of decision making? At the present time federal administrators are willing to impose higher standards of quality for the environment than those selected by some state officials. This willingness is exemplified by the arguments over nondegradation statements for water-quality standards in which EPA officials argue that state agencies should not set the further deterioration of their environments as "goals." Yet it is also true that there is considerable divergence of opinion among various state regulators. While many state officials would prefer to set lower standards than are demanded of them by federal officials, some of their counterparts would prefer to set higher ones. In disputes between state and federal officials, the latter do not always maintain the most antipollution attitudes. For example, in 1972 the state of Minnesota lost a lawsuit in which its regulatory agency argued for authority to set higher radiation-leakage standards from nuclear reactors than the Atomic Energy Commission was willing to establish.[6] Many state agencies have been infiltrated and influenced by industries that dominate the economies of their states; the national Environmental Protection Agency has likewise shown signs of yielding to pressure from nationally prominent industries such as automotive manufacturers.

There are two alternative theories, besides the notion that state people are forced by the nature of their roles to take more lenient enforcement stances, that explain any difference between federal and state officials in the strength of antipollution sentiment. First, the relative newness of the federal program may be a strong factor affecting the zeal with which its employees regard their task. The same level of antipollution sentiment may have characterized the beginnings of state-enforcement efforts. The natural history of regulatory agencies frequently commences at a high level of dedication to the public welfare. Later, however, agencies gradually tend to assume the attitudes of those regulated. This pattern of events is as likely to occur on the national as on the state level, and events surrounding the history of the Federal Communications Commission, the Federal Trade Commission, and other national regulatory agencies confirm the pattern on the national level.

Second, the timing of the federal effort may have been propitious, coming as the culmination of increasing antipollution sentiment throughout the country, among the lay public as well as among government officials at all levels. The federal effort, coming as it did at an opportune moment, gave the initial appearance of being more sincere and having behind it more dedicated personnel than state efforts. In fact, a considerable shift in official opinion at all levels of government may have occurred in the early 1970s, either causing or coinciding nicely with the new federal legislation. Recently renewed fervor for considering economic and social factors before funding or passing more abatement programs seems to be shared at all levels, too. Federal officials may well lead the retreat into a restructuring of future environmental goals along economic lines. Federal personnel, like state people, have a capacity for change that leads in two different directions. Their recent decision to postpone the attainment of air-quality goals is one indication of their responsiveness to industrial demands. Certainly they enjoy no built-in immunity to such inputs.

## POLITICAL SOLUTIONS: LITIGATION VERSUS ADMINISTRATION

In addition to the location of decision making at the federal level, a second kind of proposed change is to place greater reliance on the courts. Just as many proponents of stricter environmental controls argue for a greater federal role, so do many believe that the judiciary would prove more responsive to pleas for cessation of environmental damage. It is not unusual for persons who find themselves losing in the legislative and administrative arenas to turn to the courts to reverse the policy set by other branches of government. With the advent of the environmental lawyer and a renewed litigiousness on the part of those persons who consider themselves injured by pollution, some judges have become willing to redress the balance between the need to pollute and the need for a clean environment.[7]

Nevertheless, it is important to keep in mind the fact that the judicial branch of government had for a long time almost sole responsibility for balancing polluting and antipolluting interests in our society. And it was because of the generally conservative tendency of judges to emphasize the economic value of using the environment for dumping wastes that persons affected adversely by pollution demanded that legislatures create the administrative framework that exists today. Evidently this has proved to be a less than ideal solution. Potential violators of antipollution statutes, primarily industries and municipalities represented either by elected officials or their appointed managers, are by definition considered to be law-abiding citizens, and it is assumed that most are people of good will who genuinely wish to end pollution. Consequently, the strategy used by pollution-control officials is to ask for the cooperation of the companies or the municipalities. When, as often is the case, voluntary cooperation is not forthcoming, numerous explanations for this noncompliance are available, including technical and economic difficulties. Unlike most instances of law violation, there is little real reliance on the criminal sanction in the case of a company or municipality found discharging untreated wastes. The discharger is merely informed of the illegality of his actions and asked to modify them.

The traffic-law violator's destination or reason for being on the road is of little interest to the state patrol, but a polluter, in committing his offense, is at the same time carrying out an important function for society—producing goods for the economy or disposing of municipal wastes. Most American citizens, even antipollution-law enforcers, consider these functions, especially the production of goods, to be useful and worthwhile. Until recently many enforcers have undertaken their task almost apologetically, as if embarrassed to be interfering with such legitimate pursuits in order to enforce the law. The polluter can count more on the ambivalence of enforcement officials than can other white collar criminals.

In order to redirect administrators to their role in law enforcement, it has been suggested that environmentalists increasingly resort to private litigation. Courts have occasionally viewed favorably environmentalists' arguments that administrative agencies have not exercised all their authority in dealing with polluters; nevertheless, most of these court decisions have been directed at seeing that due process has been carried out. The courts have urged federal agencies that have not submitted environmental-impact statements before launching major projects such as building canals or issuing waste-discharge permits to do so. When questions of substance have arisen, the courts have generally still deferred to administrative judgments, as has been their tendency in the past with other types of administrative discretion.[8] Environmental lawyers are well aware of the courts' reticence to substitute their substantive judgments wholesale for those of administrative agencies. While judicial decisions may redress the grossest inequities, the administrative agencies are still responsible for the major defense of the environment.

Even it it were possible to force courts to render substantive decisions, environmentalists would have to question the wisdom of this strategy. Judges, like legislators and administrators, are influenced by their personal attitudes and values, by the values of the political culture from which they have emerged. To suggest that the courts stand as some kind of solitary advocate of a minority point of view in our society is to misread the position taken by the vast majority of U.S. judges in the past. To expect them to reflect anything other than the general attitudes toward the environment of the larger population is also unrealistic. Recent judicial decisions in favor of environmentalists is not an indicator of judges' willingness to advocate a particular cause but an indicator of the fact that judges, too, are subject to changes in opinion due to shifts in public needs and demands.

## POLITICAL SOLUTIONS: THE SUPERAGENCY

To solve the dilemma of having multiple decision makers producing policies that conflict with and sometimes counteract the effects of other decision makers, it has been suggested that environmental problems should be considered from the widest possible vantage point. By transferring decision making to a superagency that spans the functions of many individual bureaus, policy makers will be able to make trade-offs between areas and between functions now blocked by intergovernmental jealousies. The national Environmental Protection Agency, newly created overseer of the national environmental scene, is such an agency; it is currently being imitated in many states.

Problems involved in effecting this transfer of authority are numerous. Entrenched bureaucracies, in a purely defensive reaction, tend to resist the entry of another agency having greater authority over the same areas they have traditionally controlled. Only very gradually do new organizations such as EPA usually succeed in breaking down resistance to their authority. Since its creation in 1970, EPA has had problems of recognition. The administrator of the agency has pleaded for cabinet status for EPA in order to bolster its influence and image within the government bureaucracy. Future changes in the administrative structure will not eliminate problems of political influence that the administrator of EPA will have to face regardless of whether he sits in the cabinet or not. Other administrative role players, such as the head of the Office of Management and Budget and the secretary of commerce, have conflicting attitudes and interests with regard to environmental damage. Along with the strategic position that EPA may come to occupy in the future and its theoretical autonomy will subsist opponents to its policies. Some of these opponents, in OMB, for example, will occupy positions superior to EPA in the Washington hierarchy. No matter how zealous any given administrator of EPA may be, his decisions regarding environmental policy must and will be subordinate to the preferences of persons with greater influence in the executive branch.

A second problem with the superagency approach is that environmental-protection policy covers vast subjects that are as yet still poorly defined. The topics are so complex they may not lend themselves easily to comprehensive administration. If, as some advocates of pollution control wish, EPA were to be enlarged until it could effectively coordinate all environmental matters throughout the federal bureaucracy, the size of EPA itself might soon dwarf all other agencies and bureaus, thus producing the same types of interoffice rivalries and conflicts of interest that now exist between departments. The responsibilities of the present Department of Health, Education and Welfare have grown so diverse over the years that today the secretary of HEW often faces insuperable odds when he attempts to control policy making throughout his department. Suggested reforms for HEW include dividing it into its component parts—the opposite recommendation of that made for EPA. While it seems reasonable to argue that the comprehensive treatment of environmental matters must of necessity be centered in one agency, the subject matter itself is so diverse that the limits of human reasoning may be reached long before the problems are all resolved.

EPA does not yet possess either the size or the resources to adequately protect the environment throughout the United States. It continues to be dependent on cooperative actions by state and local governments and by other agencies in the federal bureaucracy. If it were ever to obtain the necessary resources and authority to act comprehensively, questions of policy direction would still remain. The history of other regulatory agencies, such as the FTC and ICC, does not encourage proponents of a strong enforcement function.

An explanation of the present bureaucracy's policy of tolerance toward pollution is necessary before attempting to debate the relative merits of projected new administrative schemes for effecting policy. As we have already noted, enforcers of present pollution-control laws prefer moral suasion over punitive sanctions. This may be due in part to the empathy that arises in a continuous face-to-face relationship between violator and enforcement official and in part to the difference in social status between middle-class governmental employees and upper-class industrialists and their lawyers. This social-status factor can only reinforce the enforcement agent's sense of uncertainty in utilizing sanctions against traditional representatives of public virtue. The transfer of this enforcement function to a superagency does not assure any changes.

Officials in the highest policy-making levels of the agency will always be selected by the president and his immediate advisors, and their attitudes toward the environment will continue to influence the decisions made by EPA, regardless of how officially autonomous it may become. Some of the criticisms of the panacea of transferring authority either to the federal level or to the court system can also be applied to the superagency concept. Personnel motivated to join a superagency would not necessarily be any more or less responsive to political pressures than those who have joined other decision-making groups in the past. EPA itself has been obviously responsive to political forces brought to its attention by administration policy makers above the agency level in the first half of the 1970s.

## POLITICAL SOLUTIONS: PUBLIC INVOLVEMENT

One final suggestion for reforming present methods of environmental protection is to involve the public to a greater extent in the deliberations of policy makers. While representatives of the public today may feed official inputs to the formal meetings of decision makers, most policy is formulated by regulatory officials in cooperation with agents of polluting groups. Together, these two sets of experts, who understand the economics and technology of pollution abatement, make the real decisions after the media and public have left the scene. To avoid this situation, lawmakers have tried to institutionalize more firmly the public's role in such processes. The newest laws on both federal and state levels make it formally possible for citizens' groups to bring court cases against government officials who they feel are not adequately enforcing the laws. Some advocates of greater controls feel that because of these laws the judicial branch of government may prove to be more favorable to the environmentalists' cause in the long run.

More open deliberations and greater public notice of impending official actions are important aspects of any democratic form of government in which the majority of citizens are supposed to be actively involved in influencing policy. Public participation is also a two-edged sword. Officials in industry are eager to become involved even more intimately in the decision-making process and have been quick to take advantage of legal provisions allowing anyone to challenge administrative decisions. Some law suits have been initiated by industry challenging the legitimacy of EPA's air-quality standards on the ground that they do not take economic and social factors into consideration.[9] The concept of opening up all administrative decisions concerning the environment to private suit may eventually prove as useful for the polluters as for those who oppose their activities. The whole problem of who wins and who loses may revolve around who can afford the better legal talent.

Eventually, too, we may have to come to grips with the problem of predicting the actual result of widening the conflict to include the majority of U.S. citizens. Most public-opinion polls on the subject have shown that wealthier, more privileged segments of the population are more concerned with clean air, earth, and water. If this finding is accurate, broadening the base of decision making may prove dysfunctional to those who wish to increase the strictness of implementation of our present laws. If the lower and middle classes become more influential, they may well prefer less esoteric values than clean air and water because of their economic constraints.

Before abandoning efforts to involve the majority of Americans in this policy area, however, it is important to consider the factors that give rise to public opinion. Given the relative ignorance of all laymen in complex technical matters, outcomes in environmental policy will depend largely on the persuasiveness of the information various interests are able to furnish to the public. The government's public-policy outputs, together with industry's private economic policies, today constitute most of the information base that the private citizen uses to understand the problem and make his choices. Industry's interest in informing the public about its position on environmental issues has increased dramatically in the first half of the 1970s. Many major firms go to great expense (tax deductible, of course) to inform the public that they are indeed concerned about environmental issues, launching massive advertising campaigns. In fact such campaigns may constitute a substantial segment of their "environmental control" budget. Even more ominous to conservationists is the new counterattack by industries such as the electric utilities, who deny the need for environmental controls. These types of ads represent the new controls as being uneconomical and too costly for society, as well as being neither effective nor technologically sound.

The lay public has little information with which to counter these arguments. It is entirely dependent on the information emanating from governmental regulatory agencies and environmental interest groups. One arena in which public-policy debate takes place is the forum of public opinion. All interests that have a continuing concern with the quality of the environment are aware of this fact. No clear-cut victory can be declared by either side in this controversy because of the passage of one law, the creation of a new agency, or the issuance of a particular court decision. The way in which the public interprets and reacts to these individual policy outputs will determine future demands fed into the political system. The selection of any framework for decision making is continually open to criticism, pressure, and change. The only truism in the debate over methods of reaching decisions is that all public policies satisfy some political actors more than others. The dissatisfied will not abandon the conflict because of one or more setbacks.

## SUMMARY

Numerous economic and political solutions to environmental deterioration have been suggested in recent years. Some critics of the present system argue that the problem is largely one of planning, or the lack thereof. Others, however, feel that governmental controls are already too onerous in this policy area. An efficient solution, in their opinion, resides in greater use of the free market to charge for the use of commonly held resources in proportion to the real value of their assimilative capacity. Despite such arguments the present tendency is to involve governmental agencies more and more intimately in the setting of environmental-policy goals. The assumption of those who advocate this course of action is the belief that if environmental decision making can be elevated to a sufficiently objective, technological level, the problems may resolve themselves. While comprehensive planning will play an increasing role in this field, the belief that there exists an optimal solution somewhere in the distance easily obtainable and visible to everyone is utopian in the extreme. Decisions made by any planning agency will continue to depend on individual values and on the quality of data available to it.

Dissatisfied interests believe that any change in the mechanism for decision making will prove beneficial to their cause and because of this commonly held belief have offered suggestions such as relocating the policy-making process exclusively in the federal government, in the courts, or in a superagency. Before making predictions of future behavior, however, political actors concerned with changing policy should first consider the fact that the personality of future policy makers is important to outcomes. As in the past, any new technique for reaching a solution will be subject to the whims of individuals and will be manipulated by all interests who feel themselves affected by those policies and able to make inputs to the policy process. The course of future environmental policy will continue to depend on the ability of opposing interests to shape public opinion, create political demands, and influence political office holders.

## NOTES

1. Edwin G. Dolan, *TANSTAAFL: The Economic Strategy for Environmental Crisis* (New York: Holt, Rinehart, 1971).
2. Howard Teichman, *George S. Kaufman: An Intimate Portrait* (New York: Atheneum, 1972), p. 127.
3. Allen Schick, "Systems Politics and Systems Budgeting," in Leslie L. Roos, ed., *The Politics of Ecosuicide* (New York: Holt, Rinehart, 1971), p. 135-158; Stahrl Edmunds and John Letey, *Environmental Administration* (New York: McGraw-Hill, 1973), especially Chs. 13–16.

4. One example of another set of experts second-guessing the conclusions reached by the initial technocrats may be found in Bruce A. Ackerman et al., *The Uncertain Search for Environmental Quality* (New York: The Free Press, 1974). In this extensive reanalysis of the decision rendered by the Delaware River Basin Commission to upgrade the Delaware River in the Philadelphia area, the authors argue that numerous faulty assumptions were made in the first analysis. The original decision was reached because of an overemphasis on the importance of the dissolved oxygen parameter, an overestimation of the likelihood of substantially increasing this parameter, and an underestimation of the costs. They conclude that the original experts erred in the direction of spending too much on pollution control.

5. An early proponent of effluent charges was Allen V. Kneese, who has written a number of books on the subject, including: *Quality of the Environment: An Economic Approach* (Washington, D.C.: Resources for the Future, 1963); *Managing Water Quality: Economics and Institutions* (Baltimore: Johns Hopkins Univ. Press, 1968). One example of the utilization of this method is described by Kneese in "Water Quality Management by Regional Authorities in the Ruhr Area," in Marshall I. Goldman, ed., *Ecology and Economics* (Englewood Cliffs, N.J.: Prentice-Hall, 1972), pp. 172–190.

6. Northern States Power Company v. Minnesota, 447 Federal 2nd 1143.

7. For some of the arguments that have been recommended by environmentalists for use in law cases, see Norman J. Landau and Paul D. Rheingold, *The Environmental Law Handbook* (New York: Ballantine Books/Friends of the Earth, 1971).

8. For a casebook that shows the direction many court decisions have taken in the past, see James Krier, *Environmental Policy and Law* (New York: Bobbs-Merrill, 1971).

9. Essex Chemical Corp. v. Ruckelshaus, No. 72-1073; Appalachian Power Co. v. EPA, No. 72-1079; Kennecott Copper Corp. v. EPA, 462 Federal 2nd 846.

CHAPTER EIGHT

# Solutions to Pollution: The Big Questions

Behind most of the specific, program-oriented suggestions for change described in the last chapter lie basic philosophical orientations toward size and growth. Most environmentalists view specific suggestions for change in the policy-making process as merely ameliorative and short-range. If any realistic solutions for the problems outlined in this book are to be found, they insist on the establishment of large-scale, comprehensive solutions—firm goals toward which other programs may be directed. From the two major causes of pollution derive the terms of these goals: population and technology, and the desirability of controlling them. Underlying most current arguments about the optimal quality of the physical environment are conflicting attitudes toward growth of either population or technology, or both. The implications behind many of the minor skirmishes in the conflict over the environment are inherent in the larger problems of our social attitudes toward population and technology.

## POPULATION CONTROL: DEFINING GOALS

If one of the factors contributing to pollution is the exponential rate of population growth, one way of tackling the problem is to restrict population increase. This is one tactic of many members of the environmental movement, particularly biologists and other natural scientists. We are face to face with the hard fact that there is finite space on our planet, and population growth must eventually cease if the present inhabitants of the earth are to continue to enjoy their lives. Less practical alternatives have been suggested, such as finding living space for our burgeoning population in outer space, but the problems of population growth that policy makers face today require more mundane measures.

Until recently the net effect of U.S. governmental policies has been to encourage rather than to discourage population growth. It is entirely possible that the majority of American policy makers and citizens prefer a constantly expanding population base. Considerations of numerical superiority have motivated many governmental decision makers throughout the world to advocate an ever-expanding population, especially during periods leading to international conflicts, and the United States is no exception. In addition to military considerations, economic policy has played a major role in encouraging population expansion. Economic advisers to presidents equate a healthy economy with a constantly expanding one and view population increase as desirable for an expanding market. Today, however, this notion is undergoing revision. Individual scientists such as Paul and Anne Erhlich and groups like Zero Population Growth are increasing their influence. Both the public and some policy makers have given some signs of accepting the new arguments for population limitation, but at present there is little consensus on the subject.

With no agreement on the population problem in sight, one of the most pressing concerns for world policy makers in the mid-1970s has become the lengthening gap between food production and population increase. The normal response to scarcity of any kind is to increase the supply rather than to attempt to control the demand. Some planners, especially those from developing nations, have argued in favor of altered patterns of consumption in the developed areas in order to provide greater quantities of protein for those now threatened with starvation. For the most part, however, policy makers in developed areas cling to the single idea of increased worldwide food production.[1] Such a solution is not a permanent one, given the limits of space on this globe. The most immediate solution to overpopulation —migration—is not a viable alternative for the technologically advanced, still relatively uncrowded countries, including the United States. Instead, it will prove to be an increasing burden as countries with the gravest imbalance between population and resources, stymied in their efforts to import foodstuffs, turn increasingly to exporting people.

If one legitimate goal of U.S. domestic policy should be to limit population growth, the question remains: What methods are available for achieving this result? The number of people living at any moment in history is dependent not only on number of births and on life span, but also on timing of births. As medical technology improves and life spans increase, only the decisions of younger people either to limit the number of their progeny or to postpone their own reproduction or both can compensate for larger numbers of older people. Two methods can achieve reduced population growth: smaller average family size and later reproduction. The average number of offspring per couple should be kept to slightly over two in order to reach zero population growth. In addition, if the average American couple were to decide to produce the next generation five years later than it does today, there would be fewer instances of four and five generations coexisting at the same time. Thus, a slight change in social patterns could be instrumental in reducing the total numbers of citizens sharing the same living space.[2]

## METHODS FOR AFFECTING POPULATION SIZE

There are several methods for achieving goals of reduced family size and later reproduction, once they are accepted. Until very recently, the United States has relied entirely upon voluntary methods of birth control to limit the rate of population growth. In nations such as China, Japan, and some Eastern European countries, apparently more concerned with their limited space and resources, governmental intervention in this problem area is already well established. In the United States, however, public policy often directly undermines the goal of limited population growth. Throughout most of U.S. history, severe legal restrictions have been imposed on abortion and on the dissemination of information on birth-control techniques. The government regarded all new citizens as valuable resources for the community rather than as liabilities who make additional demands on scarce resources. Tax exemptions exist for all members of a family, and single taxpayers and childless couples must pay disproportionately more than their fertile counterparts. Instead of being rewarded for conserving scarce resources, they are penalized for restricting their numbers.

Numerous changes have been suggested for governmental policy that might have an effect on the average family size in the United States. The first steps were taken during the late 1960s and early 1970s. First, state-imposed restrictions on disseminating birth control information that had formerly prevailed in many areas of the country were relaxed. Second, abortion laws were liberalized, first by some state legislatures and later by the U.S. Supreme Court. Discussion on this subject, however, is far from over. State legislatures continue to argue the merits and demerits of such programs. Right-to-life and planned-parenthood groups, both with vocal and active memberships, echo this debate among the populace, illustrating anew the circularity of the policy-making process.

Other alterations in governmental programs have been suggested to curtail encouragement of large families. Chief among these are recommendations that tax laws be altered to allow families a larger deduction for their first child than for subsequent children. An additional tax burden, rather than tax relief, could be imposed on those families exceeding a specified number, with special provisions for couples who take on the responsibility of raising otherwise unwanted children as their own in preference to producing their own offspring.

Governmental-spending patterns may also be utilized to affect family size and timing. Programs designed to assist families with small children may well affect individual decisions about when and how many offspring to produce. The most obvious and well-publicized example is a reduction in welfare funds for the care of dependent children. Government can also reduce funding of programs that assist middle-class and poor families in raising their children. The most vulnerable program is the public funding of education facilities. If costs for higher education continue to rise, without additional federal funding, more and more middle-class families may be forced to reevaluate the probabilities of their being able to educate their children. The average middle-class American couple who is seriously concerned about its ability to send either or both children to college, much less to graduate or professional schools, may have second thoughts about producing more than one child. Public policy on inflation and depression, and the effectiveness with which government manages to control these will obviously have an effect on population, as the lack of population growth during the 1930s demonstrated.

Attempts to control population through indirect financial pressures affect different segments of the population differentially. The poorest segments of society are hardest hit by such programs. The wealthiest are left virtually untouched and remain free to make decisions about family size and timing based on personal choice. Other suggestions have, therefore, been made, including the "1984" idea of governmental permits to individual couples for the production of children and appropriate sanctions to punish those exceeding their quotas. Such suggestions are generally considered extreme. Whether this is because direct regulations would equally affect all groups in society or because they would affect privacy and other personal liberties is an open question. Other direct methods of population control include governmental encouragement and funding of birth-control clinics. Forced or voluntary sterilization of the retarded, the poor, or those whose only offense seems to have been coming into contact with social workers has been tried from time to time.

These latter methods also discriminate against the poorest members of the population, the only ones who can be influenced by such measures to have fewer children.

Population-control programs have important implications for social, ethnic, and religious conflicts in our society. Already some view birth control and population limitation as a conspiracy to reduce the black population relative to the white. Other minority groups, ethnically or otherwise defined, which see themselves out-voted in the political arena because they lack numbers, are sensitive to this problem. Any suggestions for direct governmental attention to family size are destined to remain highly controversial.

## THE CHANGING ROLES OF WOMEN

Aside from governmental policies that may affect family size, many cultural, social, and moral considerations help to determine the number of children individual couples have. American culture, like most other national cultures, continues to reward larger families by publicity through the media and through general praise for the family unit as an institution. Men, and especially women who have never married or who have changed from married to single status, face numerous social and economic restrictions not normally put on their married counterparts. The "odd" woman at a dinner party is still a source of concern to her hostess. The career woman who wishes to negotiate a bank loan for a house mortgage is still considered a greater risk by conservative financial institutions. Recently, however, there have been some signs of changing opinion on these matters by some segments of U.S. society.

Voluntary limitation of population depends largely on women's attitudes, since they are the ones who physically reproduce the species and bear the major responsibility for nurturing the young. A shift in female roles may already have resulted in a decrease in population growth. If the women's liberation movement increases its influence in the future and women become freer to choose alternative roles to those of wife and mother, a further reduction in childbearing activity may result. To some degree, a lifestyle change is taking place among certain segments of the population even now.

In order for such a change to occur on a larger scale, however, the social attitudes of men and women must shift dramatically. Governmental policies may influence the trends toward alternative lifestyles for women through affirmative enforcement of equal-employment-opportunity legislation and equalization of legal treatment of men and women. The attitudes that public-school teachers adopt toward the socialization of girls into role types are also important. Public-policy outputs of governmental decision makers have a tremendous impact on the cultural and social environment in which the present generation of women is growing up. To say that such sensitive matters of personal, cultural, and religious decisions should be left to individual conscience is to ignore the fact that present-day policies support the current roles being adopted by women. At the present time there is some formal recognition of the need for greater flexibility in roles made available to women. Agencies such as Health, Education and Welfare, which tries to influence educational institutions to hire more women, are attempting to develop positive policies to effect these goals. But the ultimate impact of governmental policy is contingent upon future demands made by the segments of the population most intimately concerned with women's rights. Governmental decision makers seem equally capable of moving in either direction on this issue, as on the volatile abortion question.

The role that government plays in helping to determine population size is important and controversial, involving problems of economic equity, political power, and social mores. It is likely that discussions on narrow issues, such as the size of income-tax deductions, will occur more often than overt debate on the broad issue of the optimal population size for the United States. Government cannot take steps to control directly the size and timing of individual families without jarring the sensitivities of most Americans in what they have considered to be very personal matters, those affecting their deepest moral and cultural beliefs. If governmental programs do have the cumulative effect of reducing population growth or stimulating it, these programs will probably be created and maintained for other reasons. Although considerable public attention falls on problems of limitless population expansion, no coherent governmental policy restricts population growth at the present time, nor is one foreseen for the immediate future. Population policy by indirection and accident is the more likely pattern for the next decade, barring radical shifts in public opinion and/or policy making in this country.

## THE QUALITY-OF-LIFE ARGUMENT

The large family is not the only social institution presently under attack in the United States. The method we use for calculating the standard of living or the quality of life in this country has raised serious questions. Today many economists question the use of the

Gross National Product (GNP), based on the market value of all goods and services, as the single indicator of social welfare. GNP, as presently calculated, is incapable of taking into consideration some of the costs incurred by production of goods and services, such as the cost of a polluted environment. Our present economic indicators make no provision for reducing the value assigned to an automobile manufacturing plant's output by the amount it decreases the recreational use of the nearest stream, or the value assigned to real estate near a factory made less desirable by air and eye pollution or by its effect on human health. A constantly expanding GNP is not the most desirable way of calculating the success of our society. Other social indicators of the quality of life enjoyed by each citizen should be developed.[3]

Opinions vary on the most accurate method of measuring quality of life. The real problem for policy makers is to find more accurate methods of calculating the social costs of and benefits derived from production of material goods. Theorists propose very different solutions to the same problem, according to their type of calculus for estimating these factors. Some feel that the only way to achieve a more pleasing and healthful environment is to reduce our total industrial output. Others emphasize the need to redistribute present production and to emphasize certain parts of the economy over others. Those who would have us reduce industrial output argue that we have developed a throwaway economy, epitomized by such items as the nonreturnable and nondegradable container. The knowledge that the unbreakable plastic bottle that now holds our shampoo necessitates larger and larger landfills to accommodate all those discarded nondegradable containers must counter the convenience of not shattering the shampoo bottle in the shower stall. The inconvenience of a return trip with milk, pop, and beer bottles is a small sacrifice if contrasted with the litter along the highways and with the amount of available space left for landfills.

Some policy makers have seen the logic of the argument against a throwaway economy and have instituted public policies designed to reduce directly the total consumption of certain types of products. In 1973 Oregon passed a law forbidding the distribution of beverages in nonreturnable containers. The aluminum industry has vigorously attacked this particular piece of legislation, for it reduces the consumption and therefore the total production of aluminum containers. To counter this threat the industry has raised the specter of unemployment, the ultimate weapon in arguments against a conserving economy; however, the growing scarcity of certain types of nonrenewable raw materials and the enormous energy consumption in such industries as aluminum manufacture have assisted environmental interests in holding their own in this ongoing debate. Consequently, the Oregon law subsists and other states have adopted variations (for example, in Vermont) or are in the process of considering such alternatives.

Economic arguments against conservation measures are powerful. When other types of material goods are involved, the debate becomes more acrimonious, especially when the products, unlike beverage containers, are not evenly distributed throughout the population. Those of society's members who already have all the air-conditioned cars and color television sets they want or need understandably denigrate the necessity of producing more, but for those at the bottom of the ladder still waiting for their share it is crucial that the economy continue to churn out presently criticized gadgets in ever-increasing quantities, if they are to obtain a share. At the other end of the marketplace there are also problems of equity involved, even in the production of such evenly distributed goods as nonreturnable beverage containers. Workers in this industry obviously feel the pinch more than others do. Why should they be made to suffer more?

## TECHNOLOGY AS DELIVERER

It is at this point that those who argue not in favor of reducing total industrial output but of emphasizing different portions of the economy enter the debate. They argue that by restructuring the economy we may continue to employ workers at the same level or even at higher levels than that which has become politically tolerable today. A shift in emphasis from environmentally damaging aspects of the economy (disposable bottles) to environmentally useful aspects (waste-treatment plants) will accomplish this continuity of employment.

If one purpose for much of governmental spending and private investment is to provide jobs then the pollution-control sector of the economy seems equally, if not more, deserving than the pollution-creating sector. Construction of sewage-treatment plants, manufacture of smokestack scrubbers, and other expanding aspects of the pollution-control industry can employ workers thrown out of work by environmental-protection laws. Despite the well-known problems of relocation and retraining involved, the average unskilled laborer would probably be equally amenable to breaking ground for new sewage-treatment facilities or for new aluminum-production mills.

The problem of industrial pollution, as viewed from the perspective of employment, is a relatively simple one of reassessing our national priorities and redirecting public funding to the emerging pollution-control industry. If the economy can afford to make napalm for annihilating some people in order to save others from unemployment there is no economic reason why public-works projects, which have no destructive potential but seek to achieve something positive, should not also obtain the necessary funding. Particularly during economic recessions when governmental decision makers are motivated to increase public spending for the sake of prosperity, it seems only reasonable to direct the flow of funds into ecologically sensible projects. Instead of increasing the number of miles covered by public highways, the same resources could be devoted to restoring and reviving the railroad system, building mass transit systems, and funding alternative transportation programs.

The idea of altering priorities leads directly to the concept that the solution to pollution is increased technology. One solution to both the increasing volume of ordinary wastes and the creation of exotic trash unheard of in the past would be to engineer new machinery for reducing them. Until recently government and industry have failed to allocate sufficient research funds for such problems as the discovery of new methods for handling solid wastes. The solution of the difficult separation problem requires greater attention. The recovery of recyclable constituents from solid wastes and the conversion of the remainder to energy seems a desirable alternative to burial of solid wastes in the earth, where their utility is nil and where they only waste valuable space.

The notion of a more advanced technology is shared by some EPA policy makers and members of the lay public, including many of those who wish to see a cleaner environment. They advocate committing more public and private funds to research for the future goals of a pollution-free engine, more advanced methods of treating organic wastes, new methods for desulfurizing fossil fuels, and a "permanent" solution to nuclear wastes. Thus far our commitment in resources to some of these problems has been minimal. If a large-scale research program remotely comparable to that for space exploration were to be mounted, some could doubtless be solved. The vision of the United States as a nation standing hipdeep in garbage and shooting rockets at the moon remains with us.

The most obvious hindrance to a shift in priorities is political feasibility, a problem not often discussed by scientists and economists who advocate ever-escalating technological solutions. There seems little likelihood of convincing the same policy makers who for years have been willing to assess the American taxpayers billions of dollars for defense while allocating modest amounts for all domestic welfare measures combined to greatly escalate environmental spending. Arguments over the optimal level of governmental spending in general complicate suggestions for a massive public effort in pollution control. Elected policy makers have at least given considerable rhetorical, if not behavioral, commitment to reduction in the over-all budget. When campaign promises about fiscal integrity are translated into action, pollution-control measures, like other social programs such as health and education, are among the first to be cut. This is most vividly exemplified in the constant erosion of federal waste-water-treatment-plant grants, but analogous situations exist in most other areas of environmental policy.

It seems foreordained that the part of the public pie that will be drastically reduced in times of retrenchment is domestic spending and especially public-welfare measures. Those who favor environmental controls soon find themselves in competition with programs designed to ameliorate hunger, disease, and illiteracy—problems with which most ecologically sensitive individuals are also concerned. Even during periods of increased public spending policy makers do not favor innovative programs. In periods of economic recession, when demands for increased public spending occur, the simplest, most immediate solution often is to do more of the same. Economic interests, such as the automotive industry, with a large stake in the country's economic health and a large influence in the government are most likely to be heard sympathetically. Economic advisors are particularly sensitive to arguments from hard-hit segments of the economy for specific assistance. Increased spending for public highways, rather than new investment in public-transit systems, becomes not only the simplest solution, but also the politically wisest course of action.

## TECHNOLOGY AS DEMON

Problems of funding are not the only hindrances to innovative programs. Scientists and economists who consider an austerity/conservation strategy to be the only realistic long-range solution to environment problems regard refusals for new governmental research programs as blessings in disguise. Far from approving the present distribution of resources in society, however, they recommend changes in policy direction more radical than the changes of those who advocate technological solutions. Conservationists view the problem as one of producing less waste, not treating residuals after they have been produced. The problem is also one of wasting less of our natural resources, for some scientists argue that we are running out of certain essential raw materials for which there are no available substitutes, such as clean air, water, food, and land space.

The present concern over limited supplies of certain sources of energy illustrates the argument of conservationists. Technologists hasten to predict that long before the irreplaceable fossil fuels on which we have depended for so many years run out, scientists interested in this particular technology will have developed alternative sources of energy. The difficulty with this kind of solution, conservationists argue, is that a headlong rush to discover new technology often creates more problems than it resolves and does not take into account the unexpected by-products of such new discoveries.

For example, the boon to mankind of peaceful uses of nuclear energy may yet prove to be a disaster in disguise. Problems with this source of energy are numerous: catastrophic accidents that would prove immediately fatal to large numbers of people, thermal air and water pollution, and constant leakage of low levels of radiation. When considered singly for each nuclear reactor, this leakage seems insignificant. When nuclear reactors are permitted to proliferate and their cumulative radiation is considered together with the lack of information about the effects of long-range, low-level exposure to such radiation, the risk increases considerably. The problem of ultimate disposal of nuclear wastes also constitutes a matter for debate between conservationists and technologists. These wastes are now preserved in containers designed to prevent leakage and buried in the earth or at sea. Those who oppose such disposal methods argue that they will some day demonstrate the fallibility of man's capacity for creating leakproof containers, but by then it will be too late to remedy the situation.[4]

Scientists willing to depend on technology for solutions also seem willing to wait for future developments of techniques for handling present-day wastes. The scientists of the pessimistic school of thought argue that technological development has proceeded at a faster pace than the development of solutions to the problems created by technology. Scientists are morally bound to explore all possibilities for disaster by both unforeseen and predictable causes before they choose to open the entire country to the risks of any new technology.

Today, policy makers largely depend on the knowledge of experts in such matters as pollution control and energy production and conservation. They can only be confused, as is the lay public, by the conflicting advice of different segments of the scientific community. The recent debate over auto-emission controls is one such conflict. Some technocrats argue that the catalytic converters designed to control carbon-monoxide and hydrocarbon emissions will create more problems than they solve through increased production of sulfates. Others tend to minimize this newer danger, especially those who are already committed to the use of the converters. There are honest differences of opinion among scientists over the potential side effects of any new technology, and this does not make the decision makers' task any easier. Expert testimony is available for either side of any issue, ranging from testimony given by Federal Energy Administration employees to the testimony of those who donate time to the Environmental Defense Fund. Issues are not as clear-cut as policy makers would like to believe, and those who must make the final decisions for society can never shirk their responsibility by pointing to the fact that a "body of experts" has given a certain project the green light. Conflicting advice rewards any conscientious search.

The austerity/conservation school of thought argues vehemently that technological "bandaids" or after-the-fact solutions to various problems can only postpone, not prevent, catastrophe. Many substances in our physical world are finite, not the least among these being the physical space that the population can occupy. New methods of environmental control that themselves use polluting energy ultimately destroy the environment also. The only solution that such pessimistic thinkers perceive is a radical restructuring of the economy: Rather than continuing efforts to produce new devices to purify a polluted environment, they would concentrate on redirecting resources into human-oriented services, not into material goods. These persons are not insensitive to real human problems such as employment, but they argue that human talent and other types of resources should be rechannelled into the areas of recreation and human relations, not into the production of a greater abundance of material goods.[5]

The nature of the products manufactured by our society must also change. Not only should less ostentatious, lighter, more efficient car models and even public-transportation systems replace larger gas-guzzling cars; more modest means of transportation such as the bicycle or the feet should replace public-transportation systems. In the long run these might also improve the health of the majority of Americans. Such a change would necessitate a restructuring of society and a redesign of living patterns, including residential, business, and manufacturing locations. Only a very small segment of our society is prepared to consider such options at this time.

Whether or not public policy will ever be directed along these lines will depend largely on the net impact of the attitudes of individual American citizens. These attitudes in turn depend on the effectiveness of propaganda produced by all participants; from car manufacturers who call on the American consumers to have confidence in their own economy and "buy big" to environmental groups who argue for more austerity in lifestyles. Despite some exceptions found in agencies like EPA and CEQ, for the most part governmental officials reflect rather faithfully the belief in a constantly expanding economy and an escalating technology.

## CONCLUSIONS

Recent shortages in food and fuel have emphasized the fact that the world's supply of natural resources simply cannot support the current world population at the standard of living enjoyed by most Americans. It is only because the vast majority of people live at near subsistence levels that a tiny minority can afford such affluence. The international response to this crisis highlights the continuing environmental debate at the national level. Most governmental policy makers agree that the only alternative to mass starvation is to continue to increase productivity through ever more complex technology. Many academics, on the other hand, including such groups as the Club of Rome, which authorized the first study of the carrying capacity of earth, criticize this solution as bankrupt. Increased food supplies will at best postpone the tragedy unless more radical solutions are found, including ways by which the entire world population can come to live in harmony with its environment. Continuing to elevate the ambitions of the deprived majority to emulate the consumption habits of the affluent minority cannot accomplish the goal of harmony. It is a foregone conclusion that the affluents' standard of living must suffer to improve the lot of the dispossessed. Redistribution of all material goods must be effectively implemented if we are seriously to tackle the twin problems of conserving limited resources and improving the condition of the poorest people in this society and around the world.

Such problems of social justice are beyond the scope of this book, but the increasing number of natural scientists who are concerned about the limits to growth argue that the world we share is finite and has limited resources.[6] If the population continues to increase at the present rate and technology with its attendant risks struggles to keep pace with escalating needs, eventually something, somewhere, will give. Policies aimed at shaping the present and future environment are merely responses to the question: Who gets what, when, and how. The way in which policy makers respond to questions of environmental quality will have a profound effect on all American citizens in the very near future.

## SUMMARY

There is a basic division of opinion within our society about whether we ought to adopt a conserving philosophy toward natural resources or continue to place our faith in an ever-expanding economy and population base. Those who advocate the former position point to the fact that the globe on which we reside represents a finite amount of space and other resources and urge that we learn to live within its limited means, to reuse the same materials repeatedly, and to emphasize less materialistic, more humane values. Those who represent the growth philosophy place their faith in the ingenuity of human beings as an unending resource by which we may safely continue to produce more and more of the same kinds of material goods and deal successfully with the by-products after they are created. This school of thought makes little acknowledgement of the limited nature of the environment. These expanding-economy advocates point to the constant need to increase the size of the GNP in order to provide full employment for newcomers to the labor market, which in turn means an expanding market based on an ever-increasing population.[7]

Admittedly, these two positions represent attitudinal extremes. Most physical and social scientists occupy positions somewhere between the two extremes. All persons who have contemplated the options open to our policy makers at the present time have some ideas about the best allocation of resources in our society. It is doubtful that many are fully satisfied with the present mix of goods and services produced by the economy or by their current distribution among different segments of society. Given the current variety of opinions on the subject, however, governmental decision makers are not likely to take a firm stand on such large questions as the optimal size of population or the most desirable rate of economic growth.

It is more likely that decisions on specific environmental problems will continue to be made on a piecemeal, incremental basis. While such decisions will doubtless have some impact on the larger questions, our society is not about to embark on a directed course toward clearly formulated environmental goals. Any impact on the total pattern of our society will be the result of the cumulative and often accidental effect of numerous uncoordinated decisions, with all that that implies for indirection and uncertainty.

## NOTES

1. For the arguments on both sides of the problem of limited resources and increasing population see Donella H. Meadows et al., *The Limits to Growth* (New York: Universe Books, 1972); and H.S.D. Cole et al., *Models of Doom* (New York: Universe Books, 1973).

2. For a discussion of demographic trends in the world and methods for their control see Harrison Brown and Edward Hutchins, Jr., *Are Our Descendants Doomed?* (New York: Viking Press, 1972).

3. See, for example, Paul Samuelson, *Economics*, 9th ed. (New York: McGraw-Hill, 1973), p. 1951 for a discussion of the utility of Net Economic Welfare (NEW) as opposed to GNP.

4. For arguments about unclear power see Richard Curtis and Elizabeth Hogan, *Perils of the Peaceful Atom: The Myth of Safe Nuclear Plants* (New York: Ballantine Books, 1969); and Gene Bryerton, *Nuclear Dilemma* (New York: Ballantine Books, 1970).

5. Donella H. Meadows et al., *The Limits to Growth* (New York: Universe Books, 1972).

6. See n. 1.

7. For a recent review of the literature on this subject see Hazel Henderson, "Ecologists Versus Economists," *Harvard Business Review* (July–August 1973); 1–10.

## BIBLIOGRAPHY: PART 3

Ackerman, Bruce A.; Rose-Ackerman, Susan; Sawyer, James W., Jr.; and Henderson, Dale W. *The Uncertain Search for Environmental Quality.* New York: The Free Press, 1974.

Bain, Joe S., and Ilchman, W. F., eds. *The Political Economy of Environmental Control.* Berkeley: Univ. of California Press, 1971.

Baumol, William J., and Oates, Wallace. *The Theory of Environmental Policy: Externalities, Public Outlays, and the Quality of Life.* Englewood Cliffs, N.J.: Prentice-Hall, 1974.

Bohm, Peter J., and Kneese, Allen, eds. *The Economics of the Environment: Papers From Four Nations.* New York: Macmillan, 1971.

Brown, Harrison, and Hutchins, Edward, Jr. *Are Our Descendants Doomed? Technological Change and Population Growth.* New York: Viking Press, 1971.

Bryerton, Gene. *Nuclear Dilemma.* New York: Universe Books, 1972.

Caldwell, Lynton Keith. *Environment: A Challenge to Modern Society.* Garden City, N.Y.: Anchor Books, 1971.

———. *Environmental Studies.* Bloomington, Ind.: Institute of Public Administration, 1967.

Carson, Rachel. *Silent Spring.* Cambridge, Mass.: Houghton Mifflin, 1962.

Cole, H.S.D.; Freeman, Christopher; Jahoda, Marie; and Pavitt, K.L.R. *Models of Doom.* New York: Universe Books, 1973.

Commoner, Barry. *Science and Survival.* New York: Viking Press, 1965.

———. *The Closing Circle.* New York: Alfred A. Knopf, 1971.

Crocker, Thomas D., and Rogers, A. J., III. *Environmental Economics.* Hinsdale, Ill.: Dryden Press, 1971.

Curtis, Richard, and Hogan, Elizabeth. *Perils of the Peaceful Atom: The Myth of Safe Nuclear Plants.* New York: Ballantine Books, 1969.

Dales, J. H. *Pollution, Property and Prices.* Toronto: Univ. of Toronto Press, 1968.

Dolan, Edwin G. *TANSTAAFL: The Economic Strategy for Environmental Crisis.* New York: W. W. Norton, 1972.

Dorfman, Robert, and Dorfman, Nancy S., eds. *Economics of the Environment,* New York: W. W. Norton, 1972.

Dorfman, Robert; Jacoby, Henry D.; and Thomas, Harold A., Jr., eds. *Models for Managing Regional Water Quality.* Cambridge, Mass.: Harvard Univ. Press, 1973.

Ehrlich, Paul R., and Ehrlich, Anne H. *Population Resources Environment.* San Francisco: W. H. Freeman, 1970.

Garvey, Gerald. *Energy, Ecology, Economy.* New York: W. W. Norton, 1972.

Hardin, Garrett. *Stalking the Wild Taboo.* Los Altos, Calif.: Kaufman, 1973.

Heilbroner, Robert I. *An Inquiry into the Human Prospect.* New York: W. W. Norton, 1974.

Herfindahl, Orris C., and Kneese, Allen V. *Quality of the Environment.* Washington, D.C.: Resources for the Future, 1965.

Hines, Lawrence G. *Environmental Issues: Population, Pollution and Economics.* New York: W. W. Norton, 1973.

Johnson, Huey D., ed. *No Deposit—No Return.* Reading, Mass.: Addison-Wesley, 1970.

Kneese, Allen V. *Economics of Regional Water Quality.* Baltimore: Johns Hopkins Univ. Press, 1964.

———. Water Pollution: *Economic Aspects and Research Needs.* Washington, D.C.: Resources for the Future, 1962.

Kneese, Allen V., and Bower, Blair T. *Managing Water Quality: Economics, Technology, Institutions.* Baltimore: John Hopkins Univ. Press, 1968.

Krier, James E., ed. *Environmental Law and Policy.* Indianapolis: Bobbs-Merrill, 1971.

Landau, Norman J., and Rheingold, Paul D. *The Environmental Law Handbook.* New York: Ballantine Books, 1971.

McHale, John. *The Ecological Context.* New York: George Braziller, 1970.

Maddox, John. *The Doomsday Syndrome.* New York: McGraw-Hill, 1974.

Meadows, Donella H.; Meadows, Dennis L.; Randers, Jorgen; and Behrens, William W., III. *The Limits to Growth.* New York: Universe Books, 1972.

Sax, Joseph L. *Defending the Environment.* New York: Alfred A. Knopf, 1971.

Stone, Christopher D. *Should Trees Have Standing?* Los Altos, Calif.: Kaufmann, 1974.

Strong, Maurice F., ed. *Who Speaks for Earth?* New York: W. W. Norton, 1973.

Woods, Barbara, ed. *Eco-Solutions: A Casebook for the Environmental Crisis.* Cambridge, Mass.: Schenkman, 1972.

# Index